THE WRONG STUFF

By

JOHN MOORE
Commander USN (Ret.)

SPECIALTY PRESS

ISBN: 1-883809-10-X

Library of Congress Catalog Card No.: 95-72891

Text by John Moore

All photos: Property of John Moore

Published by:
    Specialty Press Publishers and Wholesalers
    11481 Kost Dam Road
    North Branch, MN 55056
    Phone: 800-895-4585

Book Trade Distribution by:
    Voyageur Press
    123 North Second Street
    Stillwater, MN 55082
    Phone: 800-888-9653
    Fax: 612-430-2211

Printed in the United States of America

INTRODUCTION

This book is not an autobiography. It's about flying airplanes and the people who fly them; about the good times and the bad; the happy times and the sad; about exhilaration and despair. It's about the joy of learning to fly, playing in the clouds, friendships which span more than fifty years, love and loss of loved ones, and about the price pilots pay for mistakes – life and death.

The wrong stuff doesn't show up just in the cockpit of an airplane but also on the drawing board, in static tests, in structural failures – and sometimes in bed. There isn't a pilot alive who hasn't done something stupid in the air, something which is eventually laughed at and talked about if he or she lives through it. That's flying.

My career spans World War II, Korea, then the Navy Test Pilot School and on to testing Mach Two flying machines such as the RA-5C Vigilante for North American Aviation before entering the space age as Manager of Test Operations for North American in the NASA Apollo program at the Kennedy Space Center.

Recently, I was looking at the first picture taken of our cadre of seven North American test pilots in Columbus, Ohio, when I joined the company in 1956. Only two of us are still alive —Ed Gillespie and I. Until a few months ago at the age of 65, Ed was still testing airplanes such as the BD-10 (a supersonic jet kit plane) because he's loony. The others were killed testing airplanes somewhere, somehow through the years. They did nothing wrong but something went wrong. In my opinion, all were better pilots than I – but something went wrong.

This book is a collection of reminiscences, remembrances, recollections, and ruminations about people I met along the way, things I saw and things which happened – too many memorial services. It's also about the individuals whose lives have touched mine in deeply personal ways. Their story as much as mine is told in the following pages.

I'm sure if I dedicated this book to any living individual I would be sued. Instead, I offer it as a tribute to them and in memory of those who lost their lives doing what they loved – flying airplanes. Many of my great friends are now resting in Arlington Cemetery, where they are saving a spot for me. Now I fly just enough to be dangerous. Look out below!

I

THE HOT PILOT

We were eating Sunday dinner in the wardroom of the newly remodeled aircraft carrier, the USS *Essex*. It was a delicious collection of steak, mashed potatoes and gravy, green peas, hot rolls, tossed salad, and coffee. After returning from a combat flight, it was rewarding to sit down to clean tablecloths, clean napkins, clean dishes and silver, and a well-prepared steak dinner. This was the gentleman's way to fight a war.

All the pilots sitting around me had been on an afternoon strike against the North Korean and Chinese Communists from our carrier in Task Force 77, operating off the eastern coast of Korea. Each had his own story to tell: Dueling with Commie anti-aircraft gunners, knocking down a railroad bridge span with a well-placed bomb, diving through clouds of flak on a bombing run to single-handedly destroy half of North Korea. We were Ernie Beauchamp's boys in Fighter Squadron 51, flying Panther jets. We thought we were pretty sharp and we talked a good fight in the wardroom.

We were in the midst of hearing Ensign Herb Graham tell how he had carefully planted a 500-pound bomb in the smoke-stack of a locomotive when our squadron duty officer dashed into the wardroom.

"I need six taxi pilots right now."

The urgency in his voice and the look on his face stopped conversation cold. Something was wrong.

"What's up, Dan?" Herb asked.

"A Banshee is in trouble and is returning for an emergency landing. Which six of you are going? Come on, he's almost back to the ship."

With silent mutual understanding, the six of us farthest along with our meal were up and on the way to the readyroom. Six of our planes were parked aft on the flight deck in the landing area, and we had to move them forward so the crippled Banshee, a twin-jet fighter, could land aboard.

Our Skipper had ordered that every time we climbed into our planes for any reason we would be in full flight gear. Sometimes that seemed like a foolish rule. Why in the world would we need all our flight paraphernalia just to start up a jet and move it forward on the flight deck? We were in a rush so I just slipped into my leather flight jacket, pulled on my helmet and Mae West life jacket, and raced topside to my plane. No gloves, no flight suit – oh well, no one would notice.

An air of solemnity engulfed the whole ship. Flight deck personnel hurried mobile starting units to our jets; plane captains were hard at work removing tie-down lines from their planes. Since word had been passed that one of our jets was in trouble, the only thing that mattered to the crew of 3,000 was the safety of the Banshee pilot. He had to be landed aboard if at all possible.

"Get those planes forward – hurry it up!" blared the bullhorn to everyone topside.

"The Banshee will be landing in three minutes."

My plane was the last one to be moved. As I crossed over the barriers amidship into the parking area forward, the bullhorn spoke crisply: "Clear deck; land the Banshee aboard."

I glanced back and saw it, a speck on the horizon, in a long straight-in approach to the ship. The taxi signalman who was giving me parking directions waved indignantly at me to follow his signals as he parked me on the very edge of the flight deck, starboard side. From the cockpit I could look almost straight down to the green-blue water some seventy feet below.

After shutting down the engine, I unbuckled the safety belt, took off my helmet, and started to climb out of the cockpit. The shriek of the crash whistle pierced the air. My head jerked around to see what was happening. The Banshee had touched down on the flight deck at more than 130 knots and its hook had failed to engage an arresting cable. It bounced high into the air, cleared the crash barriers designed to stop it in case of an emergency, and was bearing down on my plane at an incredible speed. I glanced at the water moving swiftly below the bow of the ship. I knew there was going to be a crash, and I had a fraction of a second to decide whether to jump from my plane. It wasn't time enough. Wrong!

There was a poof, like a blowtorch being ignited, then fire – fire everywhere. I saw the tremendous billow of deep red flames and black smoke for an instant before the heat triggered my reflexes and locked my eyelids closed. I could feel my plane tumbling on its side onto the catwalk. The heat was horrible. I dived with all my might out of the cockpit and felt myself falling, still in this ball of fire.

"Well, this is it," I thought to myself as I seemed to keep falling through space. What a way to die: falling ... falling ... then nothing.

Suddenly, I popped to the surface of the water like a cork, with no recollection of hitting the water or swimming underwater. I could hardly believe I was alive. That water felt wonderful, soothing and cool. The huge, gray hull of the ship was no more than ten feet away and moving at more than twenty knots. Instinctively, I pulled the toggle on my life jacket and it quickly inflated. My hands! My God! They were fried. The water felt so cool on them. Then a wave of burning gasoline on the surface of the water swept down on me. Damn it! I had inflated my life jacket and could not swim underwater. Wrong again.

The Navy's survival program began paying dividends. Remembering the splashing swimming stroke taught to Navy pilots for swimming in water covered with burning oil or gasoline, I commenced splashing a path away from the aircraft carrier. As I splashed and swam, the fire on the water started moving farther and farther away from me in all directions. I looked around and saw that I was encircled by a ring of fire at least fifteen feet in diameter.

"Hey!" a voice called out.

"Hey down there!"

I looked up and saw our ship's helicopter hovering about eight feet above me. The helicopter was blowing the fire away from me, and all the time I thought I had been doing it with my superb swimming.

Lieutenant Charlie Jones, the helicopter pilot, hovered his whirlybird right over me, and his crewman in the rear seat lowered the sling to the water. I climbed in and was hoisted up to the edge of the cabin. The crewman reached out for my hand to pull me in as I yelled, "For God's sake, don't touch my hands. How does my face look, Charlie? Does it look bad? How badly am I burned?"

Charlie didn't say a word. He spun me around, grabbed me by the seat of my pants and eased me into the rear seat.

"How does my face look?" I asked the crewman in the rear seat. "Is it very bad?"

"You'll be okay, sir," he said. He was white as a ghost. My face felt stiff and numb. I looked at my hands again. They were raw. I was concerned about my face and head. All my life I'd been afraid of being scarred, and now I guessed the worst.

We were making a landing aft by the number three elevator. The forward end of the flight deck was a blazing inferno. Charlie sat her down very gently and eager arms reached up to help me from the helicopter.

"Don't touch me. I'll get out myself."

I stopped and sat on the edge of the seat.

"Thanks a lot, Charlie. You sure did a nice job and I ..."

"Get the hell out," interrupted Jones. "There are some more guys in the water I've got to get."

After the crash Charlie had seen several men in the water – one immediately imperiled by burning gasoline on the surface – and his first thought had been to fly his helicopter down over the swimmer and blow the fire away from him with the strong downwash from the rotors while he effected the rescue. He had maneuvered his helicopter underneath the outrigging antennas on the starboard side of the ship, coming to hover over me so close to the hull that the tips of his whirling blades had been only a few feet from the ship's side. It turned out there were six or seven men in the water. Charlie pulled two out and the helicopter from the USS *Boxer* got one more. The others were either too badly burned to survive or were fatally injured in the fall to the water and were not recovered. Jones' crewman was on his first helicopter assignment. It was also his last. He would never fly again.

Several sailors were helping me down the flight deck when three more ran up with a wire stretcher. Lying down on the stretcher I looked up into the face of P.E. Hall, AD1, an aviation mechanic from our squadron.

"How's my face, Hall? Am I badly burned?"

"Naw, you look fine, Mr. Moore. You're going to look as good as ever in a few days."

Good old Hall. He was one of the nicest and most convincing liars in the squadron.

The side deck elevator lowered my contingent of aides and myself to the hangar deck, and there commenced one of the most hectic trips of my life. The hangar deck is always crowded with parked airplanes and I wondered how my stretcher-bearers were going to weave through the maze of planes and criss-crossed tie-down cables to sick bay far aft on the second deck. The answer came quickly. They hustled their load of burned pilot up to the first plane, placed the wire stretcher gently on the steel hangar deck, gave it a hard shove and it sped swiftly but surely under the plane between the wheels to waiting arms on the other side of the plane.

"For Pete's sake, let me out of here; I'll walk back to sick bay!"

"You're okay, Mr. Moore, don't worry a bit."

Hall's words were not reassuring. I felt like a disc on a shuffleboard court. Hall was right; the trip to sick bay, though harrowing, was successfully accomplished in amazing time.

I was placed in the operating room with two sailors who were being treated for wicked looking burns. More injured were being carried in. It was somewhat astounding to think that I had dived from the flight deck into the water, been rescued by a helicopter, returned to the flight deck and stretchered to sick bay. It had all happened so fast that I was one of the first to arrive for medical treatment.

Two corpsmen approached, followed by a doctor. After covering me with blankets, the corpsmen carefully started scissoring up the left sleeve of my flight jacket.

"Hey, cut that out. This is my new flight jacket," I said.

"Sorry, sir," one of them said quietly, "but we don't want to pull the jacket off over your hands."

I could see their point. I glanced at the new leather jacket. It was burned all the way through in several places and was a mess. Off came the wet jacket and shirt, and although the blankets felt awfully good, I began to feel very cold and began to shake all over. The doctor, who was hanging a bottle of plasma on the bulkhead next to my stretcher, said, "The chill is normal, don't worry about it. It comes from shock."

"I think it's coming from my wet pants, doc," I said.

The blanket hid that part of my torso, and they had forgotten about the pants. With the wet clothes off, the chill disappeared and I was more comfortable.

The question of the day was foremost in my mind again.

"Doc, how badly is my face burned? Will I be scarred?"

"I don't know yet. It's too soon to tell, but I think you'll be all right."

The doctor and corpsmen started applying pressure Vaseline gauze bandages to my hands and head. In less than an hour, my hands and arms were completely encased in pressure bandages that were the size of huge boxing gloves, and my head and face were completely wrapped and covered. Only a small slit was left across my eyes, and a narrow opening over my terribly tender burned lips.

Close examination revealed a small, light burn in the middle of my back and another on the right cheek of my buttocks. I wondered how I had gotten burned there.

I was taken across the passageway, plasma bottle and all, to a small, four-man room equipped with two double bunks. Soon another pilot was brought in with one side of his head and one hand bandaged. He was Ensign Dale Bauer of VF-172. Dale had just parked his plane and was walking back to the readyroom when the careening Banshee passed inches over his head, crashed and exploded. He was caught in the edge of the fire and ran out of it. Within thirty minutes a third pilot was carried in. He was Ensign Mick Sluis, also of VF-172. He had parked his plane and climbed out when he saw the Banshee coming. He ran to the edge of the flight deck and was engulfed in the mushroom of fire from the explosion. He dove into the water and almost drowned before he was picked up by a helicopter. He was so weak when he got into the helicopter sling that he passed out, and the helicopter crew had been unable to get his limp, six-foot,four-inch frame into the cabin. They left him dangling in the sling below the cabin as they flew up to the flight deck.

Mick's arms and head were bandaged the same as mine. We occupied the two bottom bunks; Bauer had the upper bunk over Sluis.

On the flight deck the fire, fed by high-octane fuel from the burning jets (each one held almost 1,000 gallons), raged for more than an hour before fire-fighters were able to extinguish it. Eight jets were demolished in the conflagration.

In sick bay, fifteen men lay burned or injured. Doctors and corpsmen were busy every minute tending their patients, some burned almost beyond recognition. The ship's chaplain came into our room while Sluis and I were busy consuming our second bottles of plasma.

"How do you feel, Moore?" asked Chaplain Morton.

"Not too bad, Padre. We dope addicts feel no pain you know." The morphine helped.

"Padre, how did the pilot of the Banshee make out?" I asked, fearing the answer.

"We don't know yet, John," he answered very softly. I could tell by his voice and the look on his face that he knew but didn't want us to know.

We asked him to say a prayer of thanks to God for having spared our lives. The three of us felt deep appreciation that we were alive.

The entire aft end of the ship was permeated by the stench of burned flesh which came from sick bay. The flow of visitors to see injured shipmates was minimized and controlled not by the medics, but by only one requirement: the possession of a strong stomach.

About 2100, almost three hours after the accident, the door to our room opened slowly and in came my very close friend and roommate, Lieutenant Tom Hayward. Looking down at Sluis and myself in the two lower bunks, he couldn't tell which was which.

"Hi, Tom," I said to help him identify me.

"How are you feeling, John?"

"Could be a lot worse."

"You always told us you were the hottest pilot in the fleet, old man," jibed Tom, "but you didn't have to go to such extremes to prove it."

It was becoming more difficult to talk, and I was not able to see Tom very well. I could see all right when the helicopter had picked me up, and I seemed to remember seeing okay in the operating room. Now, I was worried about my eyes.

After a short visit, Tom left quietly and I immediately called a corpsman.

"Would you please hold a magazine in front of me?" I asked him. "I want to see if I can read it."

"Do your eyes hurt, sir?"

"They don't actually hurt, but I can't seem to see clearly."

He held up a magazine and to myself I read, "The comnissin secks to roll up veleose ot funds."

"Read the top sentence of that paragraph to me slowly, will you please?" I asked the corpsman.

"Mr. Moore, you're tired and doped up. Why don't you forget it until tomorrow?"

"Come on, read it. Please."

"Okay. It says: 'The commission seeks to hold up release of funds.'"

"I'll be damned."

The realization that perhaps my vision had been permanently impaired and that my face might be badly scarred began to counteract the feeling of gratification for being alive.

The night wore on slowly and restlessly. A midnight snack of codeine and sleeping pills helped the early morning hours to pass.

A steady vibration from the ship's screws shaking my bunk awakened me. I tried to open my eyes to see what was the matter. They would not open.

"Corpsman! Corpsman!" I called anxiously.

"What's the matter, Mr. Moore?"

"I can't open my eyes. Take a look at them."

"They are swollen shut, sir. But I believe that's to be expected. They may be that way for several days."

Bauer was feeling pretty good, but Sluis was still very quiet. Breakfast was served about 0630. Bauer had to keep me posted as to what came in and went out of our room. I was a very curious blind man.

The corpsman fed Dale his breakfast – two eggs over easy, coffee and pastry. The doctor fed me mine – saline solution and plasma, taken intravenously.

During the next few days, our room was visited by all our friends aboard. We learned that three men had been killed in the accident, including the pilot of the Banshee, and four more were missing and presumed lost. Fifteen of us lay in sick bay with various degrees of burns, including one sailor whose body was more than seventy percent covered with second- and third-degree burns and who was barely clinging to a few thin threads of life.

On Thursday morning, the *Essex* was steaming toward Yokosuka for a much needed rest for her crew and repairs to the starboard catapult and flight deck. Sluis was in better spirits now after a few disheartening days. His eyes were open and he was off intravenous feeding. This was my day, too. Like a baby puppy, my eyes were beginning to open at last. I could see light and make out shapes. And through straws placed with great care between swollen lips, I was drinking fluids.

Friday afternoon we were just hours away from mooring at Piedmont Pier, N.O.B. Yokosuka, Japan. My eyes were open enough that I could see and identify people.

In midafternoon I was out of my bunk for the first time since the night of the accident. With the help of two corpsmen I walked back into the operating room for a complete change of bandages. It took more than an hour to unwrap the yards of Vaseline gauze and rewrap the burns again in more pressure bandages. It was a tedious hour. The new bandages left my face exposed but covered my neck, head and chin.

For a week I had been worried about what my face looked like. On the trip back to my bunk, my two amiable crutches led me to a mirror for a look. One glance and I knew why our visitors had been nauseated when they saw Sluis and me.

It was dark when the ship moored to Piedmont Pier. The three of us were carried in stretchers off the ship to waiting ambulances on the dock, then transported to the Naval Hospital at N.O.B. Yokosuka. I was placed in a room by myself; Bauer and Sluis occupied a suite down the passageway. I must have smelled the worst to rate such privacy.

The first night in the hospital at Yokosuka produced a new flavor of medical treatment: nurses. The night nurse delivered my evening assortment of pills; there were almost enough to play acey-deucy. The pain killers and sleeping tablets fought their way past the less energetic pills in my stomach to lull me into a deep sleep; a sleep which lasted until the duty thermometer pried up a heavy tongue and nestled itself comfortably in my mouth at 0630 in the morning. The thermometer was followed closely by the pill man who was then followed by a breakfast tray. She put the tray down, then gave me the warmest, sweetest smile I had seen in years. Her name was Mary, but she was so tiny she was known as Sukoshi, and everyone was in love with her.

Dr. Caulkins had decided to treat our burns by exposure to the air and ply us with cortisone to help the body build new skin. Monday he was to take off our pressure bandages. Meanwhile, each of us consumed some two- to three-dozen assorted pills a day – Aureomycin to fight infection, codeine to ease pain, and little pills to keep the big pills company.

13

Monday morning the pressure bandages came off. First from the head – that was easy – then the right hand. Removal of the bandages went all right until Dr. Caulkins got down to the last few layers. Then it began to pull. The closer he got to the flesh, the more it hurt, until the pain became almost unbearable. The healing flesh had started to grow through the mesh of the bandage in spite of the Vaseline, and the process of removing it was as painful as getting burned. Sukoshi held my French-fried head and patted me gently as I swore unashamedly. After taking off the bandages on the right hand, the doctor knew I'd had it for this day.

Part of Dr. Caulkins' plan was for the three of us to soak our hands in tubs of water warmed to 100 degrees F twice a day. After breakfast and after lunch we were delivered in wheelchairs to Physiotherapy, where for twenty minutes at a time, we gently swirled our hands in this warm water. We were told to try to bend our fingers after the water had soaked the sterile towels from our hands. It was hard work. My fingers were stiff as boards, and at first I could not seem to move them. Progress was amazing, however. In a couple of days I could move each fingertip almost an inch.

My entire face had turned black with a heavy crust that extended into my scalp and made my scattered hairs look like sprigs of dried up grass planted in black topsoil. It almost broke my heart.

We had learned that the medics, when talking to one another, called the three of us "the burns." The young Marine officer in room 215, whose leg had been blown off by a land mine was called "the amputee." The lieutenant in 218 was "the hernia." The officer across the passageway from me had his head cut to pieces in a helicopter crash in Korea. Shaved and all stitched up, it looked like a baseball. He was "the skull," naturally.

A Marine officer was brought in and placed in room 221. We found out he had been recovering from a lower abdominal operation in a Korean hospital when an infection had set in and drained into his testicles. We figured to have a field day with the nurses on this one. Finally, my victim entered.

"Say, Betty, I have a question."

"Shoot," she said.

"We know you medics call us all by our ailments. You call us 'the burns,' and down the way are 'the amputee' and 'the hernia.' What do you call the Marine officer who just moved into 221?"

Calmly she replied, "We call him 'the Major'."

14

Betty was a buxom, outgoing gal who was as earthy and cheerful as Sukoshi was sweet and tender. Betty usually gave me my daily bath in bed, which involved maneuvering the top sheet to cover personal parts as she scrubbed the rest of my body. As she put it, she washed down as far as possible and washed up as far as possible, then had a male corpsman come in to wash "possible." Her words.

During our third week in the Navy Hospital in Yokasuka, I discovered I was still a man. Since the fire, I had not had a single sexual thought and everything had lain dormant as if there were nothing there. Betty changed that, by happenstance, I think.

She was busy washing up toward my personal area and had my knees bent to facilitate the exercise. Suddenly, I felt the washcloth washing things that were normally saved for later, and was aware of an awakening thereabouts. She could see all of this, which for me was an inordinate embarrassment. It only occurred to me later to be jubilant that this thing was working again.

Then came the trauma.

Betty said, "I'll send the corpsman in to finish up," and departed.

I didn't know what to do. The corpsman would come in and there would be a lot more to wash than he had been washing. While I was trying to figure out how to hide this thing, the mini-crisis was resolved by another corpsman who came in to give me my daily dose of cortisone in the butt, administered by a six-inch syringe and a three-inch needle. One look at that bastard and any thought I might have had of procreation dissolved into nothingness. Moments later, the bathman came in and needed only minimal soap and water to wash "possible."

The next day, Betty came in laughing loudly and asked, "How'd it go yesterday?"

We did have a good laugh and by now everyone on Ward H knew. Funny. As she walked out, she turned and said, "John, you are recovering wonderfully. If you grow new skin any faster, you'll have to be circumcised again before you leave." She laughed all the way down the hallway. Great broad.

We had been told by Dr. Caulkins that "the burns" would be evacuated by air as soon as we were well enough to travel. So, I promised all my friends that I would take care of their wives and keep them from being lonesome. They weren't worried; I was a picture of repulsion. Negative sex appeal, I think the boys called it.

By constantly exercising my fingers, they became more and more agile. One day I touched my thumb and forefinger together. It was a real triumph. The thick, black scales started peeling piece by piece from my face. Underneath was bright pink skin, tender as tissue paper. One day a big piece came off of my forehead, leaving it almost clear of dead skin. I looked in the mirror.

"It's gone! Dale, it's gone!"

"What's gone?" asked Bauer.

"My birthmark! Don't you remember the big, brown birthmark on the left side of my forehead about an inch long and half-an-inch wide?"

"Sure, I remember. Let me see," said Bauer. "Well, I'll be damned. It IS gone!"

My recovery was progressing at a good pace now. The ugly black crust was almost gone from my face just a month after the accident. Exactly twenty-five days after the big accident I could touch all my fingers to my thumb. It was a glorious day when I wrote my first letter home. It was a collection of scribbled words, barely readable, but I could not have been more proud of it had it been a Pulitzer Prize-winning novel.

Dr. Caulkins told us we would be sent home for further hospitalization as soon as we could dress and take care of ourselves. We could get into our clothes, but because our fingernails were all coming off, we could not button any buttons. Bauer had the only good hand between us, and it still had some healing to do. With the help of the corpsmen we could put on our uniforms for trips to Ship's Service and the "O" Club. Once buttoned into our clothes, we were there to stay until some kind soul undressed us. Consequently, all trips had to be carefully planned. Something we discovered the first evening we went to the club. We'd had about three beers apiece when it became apparent that our situation was critical, and the evening's activities ended abruptly as we returned to the hospital for help.

After five weeks at the Naval Hospital, Yokosuka, we were ambulanced to Haneda Airport outside of Tokyo and boarded an Air Force air evacuation plane bound for home. We wore uniforms and new, bright pink skin, which was far more tender than any newborn baby's.

Our plane transported fifty-one patients, all in litters, to San Francisco. Many were not ambulatory, and across from me was one of the most handsome young men I'd seen in years. Great smile, great attitude, but missing his left arm and left leg. Land mine, God damn it. Stupid war.

At Mare Island Naval Hospital in San Francisco, we were permitted to select any military hospital in the country for further hospitalization. Sluis and Bauer chose Chicago; I requested Balboa Naval Hospital in San Diego where my lovely wife and two boys were waiting for me.

Bidding goodbye to my compatriots, I boarded a train for San Diego and a reunion with my family. My concern for what they would think of my warmed-over ugliness mounted throughout the trip south along the California coast. My hair was growing back scraggly and with a brackish-green hue; my ears were encased in Vaseline gauze bandages, which looked like handles on a sugar bowl; my face and neck were a very bright pink; my hands were brilliant red and generously landscaped with large blisters. I was truly the man of extinction. Without any doubt, I was bringing home the wrong stuff.

The train backed into the San Diego station, and I could see Marilynn and the boys from my window. They watched closely as the passengers disembarked, not knowing what to expect.

As I stepped off the car, three-year-old Randy, who hadn't seen me in months, cried out, "Mommy, there's Daddy!"

The big hero returning from the war cried like a baby.

The "Hot Pilot" was home.

But time has been good to me. My hands are still wrinkled and tender as I write in 1995; my hair is white instead of green; I have half an ear which is easily concealed by a hair stylist. I hide my funny looking, scarred upper lip behind a sloppy looking moustache, and my kids love me. What else is there? Bauer is fine and lives in Vero Beach, Florida. I've lost track of Sluis. My helo rescue pilot Charlie Jones runs Norman, Oklahoma, and my great and patient roomy, Tom Hayward, became Chief of Naval Operations in 1978, to nobody's surprise. And if you want to know who was the Navy's hottest pilot, ask Tom Hayward!

II

SURVIVING THE CUTLASS

The Cutlass was one of the more memorable airplanes I flew in my years as a hooker. In fact, it was unforgettable. As my friend Ed Gillespie, fellow Cutlass driver, said, "periods of excitement interspersed with moments of stark terror." At the gray-hair stage in life, my recollections of details may be fuzzy but not so of events in surviving the Cutlass. Unfortunately, I seem to be touched by that memory disease, the name of which escapes me at the moment, so I respectfully ask the indulgence of those few surviving heroic Cutlass drivers if my statistics are suspect.

In the summer of 1953, after two tours with VF-51 in the Korean thing, Bob Rostine and I were dispatched to the Naval Air Test Center, Patuxent River Naval Air Station, Maryland, at the instigation of our great Skipper, George Duncan, who as it turned out, seemed to be punishing us for something. Rostine, one of the finest stick-and-throttle jocks who ever lived, went straight to the Carrier Suitability Branch of Flight Test, where they needed a pilot with his skills to take the F7U-3 Cutlass carrier trials tests. I went to Test Pilot's School, Class 11.

Rostine could make any airplane, in fact any moving vehicle, look good. He could have saved the Edsel. If anyone could make the Cutlass look good, he could. He did. Bob was a Reserve officer who had applied a number of times for Regular Navy. Why he had not been accepted, no one knew. But he made the Cutlass look so good aboard ship that Chance Vought hired him away from the Navy. Probably the brightest move Vought ever made.

Rostine's boss, Paul Thayer, a former Cutlass pilot, had put on one of the best air shows ever at Pax River flying the F7U-1. He had roared in low over the field during a scheduled air show and pulled up into a vertical climb to the cheers of thousands. Toward the top of the ascent, the entire aft end of the Cutlass burst into flames, followed by Thayer ejecting safely to the field below while the Cutlass Roman-candled into Chesapeake Bay in a glorious display of pyrotechnics. That was Thayer's last flight in the Cutlass, which showed how smart he was and why he made president of Ling Temco Vought.

Rostine went on to become Chief Test Pilot of LTV and was, until the day he died of cancer, one of the very best.

I made it through Test Pilot's School and in spite of being low man on the scrotum pole, was assigned to Carrier Suitability, joining a small if innocuous group which included the likes of Nick Smith III, Al Shepard and Rostine, under the tutelage of our Skipper, Bob Calland, with John Shepherd providing vast quantities of empirical data to which no one paid any attention.

While Al Shepard and Smith were frolicking about in A4Ds, F4Ds, F9F-8s, F3Hs and the like, I was assigned to two rather diverse programs. One was backing up Rostine in the Cutlass, since he would soon be joining Chance Vought. The other was the Flexdeck Program, which involved making wheels-up arrested landings onto a rubber deck after John Norris of Grumman had demonstrated it could be done, for whatever reason. The Air Force had made two arrested landings onto a rubber deck using a straight-wing F-84 as the test vehicle. The first one had caused serious injury to the pilot's back, so they got another pilot for the second landing, which caused serious injury to the pilot's back. With the admirable wisdom of a tailhookless Air Force, they abandoned the project. The Navy, however, persevered, believing that with their superior pilots in fold, Naval aviators could do on the pitching deck of an aircraft carrier what Air Force pilots could not do on a stationary air field.

As I was roaring around the carrier pattern in AD-5Ns during the carrier suitability trials on USS *Coral Sea* (CVA-43), Rostine was completing the Cutlass carrier suit tests. He made the Cutlass look like something Donald Trump would buy. That's when Chance Vought hired him and I was assigned the F7U project as Smith and Shepard busied themselves out of sight until the deed was done. No wonder Al became an astronaut and Nick Smith head of the Test Pilot's School – they were smarter than I was by a bunch.

In the carrier suit stable was a collection of airplanes instrumented to measure stress parameters associated with catapult and arrested landing operations. Thus the carrier suit pilots, seven or eight of us, would frequently be dispatched in the instrumented flying machines to calibrate newly installed launch and landing equipment on various aircraft carriers. That made for a lot of diverse carrier operations, such as Project Steam, aboard *Hancock* (CVA-19), based in San Diego. For Project Steam, we took all our instrumented carrier suit planes from Pax River to North Island to evaluate and help calibrate *Hancock's* new steam catapults. I was first to depart in F7U-3 BuNo. 128475, and last to arrive by several days, after lots of hydraulic fluid and JP-5 jet fuel. But I got there, nonetheless. Supplementing our stable were a few other uninstrumented flying machines and pilots, including Floyd Nugent in another Cutlass.

One of Floyd's F7U flights was impressive. As he was catapulted, the landing gear oleos extended as he became airborne, extending one of the mains to the bottom of the Pacific, about 6,000 feet deep at that point. Landing the Cutlass on land or sea was normally a memorable event under the best of circumstances, but without a main landing gear or wheels-up, dicey at best. So Floyd trimmed up at 8,000 feet under the watchful eye of Nick Smith in an FJ-3 and punched out some thirty miles offshore from San Diego. Good parachute, good water landing, good helo pickup and Floyd was deposited at the North Island Naval Air Station. Meanwhile, the Cutlass did not seem to miss Floyd one whit and just kept on going. Soon it headed east toward San Diego, pursued by Nick Smith, who had discovered that this Cutlass had exceptional perseverance. Nick made several valiant attempts to tip the wayward airplane seaward by putting his wing under the stubborn F7U, gaining for his efforts only smashed-up running lights. The Cutlass could have cared less.

Floyd looked up from the helo pad at North Island only to see a Cutlass, sans canopy, flying by. He wondered who was flying it and the answer was: no one. In fact, it seemed to fly as well without Floyd as with him.

After a simulated rocket attack on Pt. Loma and an exciting simulated strafing run on the Hotel Del Coronado, the Cutlass hung ten on a wave just south of the Hotel Del, coming to rest about fifty feet offshore amongst the startled abalone, many of which had never seen a Cutlass.

Fortunately, the call for more wheels-up rubber deck landings at Pax River was loud enough for me to S2F it across country with Bob Feliton, Marine type, ending my F7U venture on *Hancock*.

Shortly afterward, when old No. 475 was returned to Pax River, our Skipper decided that at least one of our Landing Signal Officers (LSO) should be checked out in the Cutlass – familiarity and all that. Bill Tobin of the handle-bar moustache was selected – no volunteer he – and after adequate brief-ings, we went down to the Cutlass for "Tobe's" first familiarization hop. Following yet another cockpit tour, Bill, strapped in and ready, started both engines. As they idled, he observed that two of the four flight control hy-draulic system warning lights were blinking on and off – mostly on.

"Why," he asked, "are these lights on?"

I assured him there was nothing to be concerned about – just a pecu-liarity of this particular airplane.

"How," he asked, "does one shut the engines off?"

I showed him, wherewith he shut down both engines, unbuckled, pushed me and himself down the access ladder, and walked away. He never again got in the Cutlass, or under it, for that matter.

Most of us agreed the Cutlass could be made into a pretty good fly-ing machine with a few modifications, like adding a conventional tail, tri-pling the thrust, cutting the nosewheel strut in half, completely redoing the flight control system, and getting someone else to fly it. It was, indeed, one of the first fighters with a completely irreversible flight control system – it actually had four separate hydraulic systems to power the flight controls. But it was really an unreliable, unforgiving airplane, and was helped none at all by Westinghouse's J46 engines, which generated about the same amount of heat as their toasters. From the flying standpoint, for example, Bob Rostine, in briefing me early on, explained that as you approach the stall in clean configuration, the Cutlass felt as if it were slicing to the left through the air, and suggested that I become familiar with the sensation, which I did. Sure enough, a discernable slice. One of the other indomitable F7U drivers at Pax River pursued the slice one day and suddenly found himself in a post-stall gyration from which he could not recover. He leaped out safely at about 5,000 feet into the chilly Chesapeake Bay as his Cutlass splashed below.

"How could this be?" thought Bud Sickle, a fine pilot with a bunch of F7U hours, flying with a RAG unit out of Moffett or somewhere.

"I'll take a look at it," says he. Sure enough, the slice, the post-stall gyration, the ejection, the parachute blossoming above. Two for two.

Chance Vought said, "Wait a minute, we'll look at this."

They instrumented one of their F7Us at Dallas for the test, put a cam-era in the cockpit that focused on the pilot, somehow found one of their pilots who would fly the mission (not Rostine, you can bet), and off they went: well documented flight test. Approach to stall, data on, camera on, the slice, the post-stall gyration, excellent movies of great activity in the cockpit – right stick, back stick, forward stick, then both hands up to the face curtain. A firm pull and there was no one in the cockpit. Three for three. Cutlass pilots, those who were left, were admonished to avoid the post-stall gyration.

At Pax, we were advised to prepare for the arrival of a new model of the Cutlass, which was the F7U-3M, configured to carry four Sparrow missiles, with more fuel, much more gross weight, but no more thrust. Same Westinghouse windmills, two J46s, each supposedly generating 6,000 pounds of thrust in afterburner, and about 3,500 pounds in military rated thrust (MRT). Of course, there was no modulation to the afterburners – either on or off. Full-up gross weight with four Sparrows was in excess of 32,000 pounds, with landing weight ranges of 24,000 to 25,000 pounds when returning aboard with the four missiles and a reasonable fuel reserve.

I managed somehow to convince our Skipper that I had served my time in the Cutlass and that some other lucky lad should have the opportunity to share the exhilaration I had known. Sure enough, a new and unsuspecting graduate of the Test Pilot School, Class 13 I think, named Johnny Long was assigned to -3M. Johnny was a neat guy, always smiling, always eager. I never flew the F7U-3M at Pax while Johnny was preparing for carrier trials on Shangri-La (CVA-36) out of San Diego, but I bid him well as he departed in his -3M for the West Coast via Marietta, Dallas, and El Paso. Unfortunately, as Johnny landed at Dallas next to the Chance Vought plant, he lost it after touchdown. The airplane rotated counterclockwise and slid to the left off the runway, shearing all three landing gear. The plane did not burn, and Johnny managed to get out safely, but was badly incapacitated with a broken back.

My exhilaration of knowing that Johnny was alive, if bent, was short-lived as I was advised of my newest assignment: the F7U-3M project. I do believe that was the first "oh shit" of my flying career.

When the replacement -3M was ready at Vought, I was dispatched via commercial airline to Dallas, dressed in my clean uniform. The pall of the event was only assuaged by the adulation of the stewardii and their admiration for both my ribbons. Arriving in Dallas, first things first – a visit to the hospital to see Johnny Long.

I found him lying on a curved slab, bent backwards pretzel-like, with his stomach at least a foot above his head and feet. The medics were trying to reposition some vertebrae before encasing him in plaster from head to toe. Ever-smiling Johnny – God, I don't know how he did it. Nice but brief visit (always be brief in hospitals). He did not know what had happened or how he lost it.

"You look great, Johnny." (He didn't.) "Bye."

After some briefings by the Chance Vought pilots (they had some great pilots along with Rostine), I prepared for my first visit with the -3M.

"We always take off in afterburner," they said.

It did not take long to find out why. After getting airborne and checking systems – it seemed like just another Cutlass, if sluggish – I came in to shoot some simulated carrier landings and encountered my first anomaly. (Chance Vought used that word frequently.)

While making my approach from the 180 about 100 feet over the rooftops, and at an acceptable approach speed, i.e. 135 knots, I found that I was at full Military Rated Power trying to maintain airspeed. It was not enough. At the 90 in a lovely approach, my airspeed was rapidly decreasing to such an extent that I went into afterburner to accelerate out of the Dallas Econo Lodge. Once up to 150 knots, I resumed the simulated carrier approach, finding myself at MRT again just to stay airborne. The landing was uneventful, it turned out. I made four more approaches and landings, according to my log book, and each time I was forced to use afterburner to make it around the pattern. It was troubling.

Lengthy discussions of this problem with Chance Vought types, including the pilots, resulted in two things: (A) Yes, the plane had a thrust problem, which the Vought pilots accommodated with a faster, descending approach, and usually at lighter gross weights than I was going to be required to use; and (B) they agreed to do engine calibration runs to assure the J46s were properly set. From the latter there was bad news, and there was bad news. The first bad news was that, indeed, the right engine temperatures were incorrect, and the other bad news was that the temps were too high and in resetting them downward to correct limits, I lost another couple hundred pounds of thrust at MRT.

Another anomaly evolved that would ultimately throw fear into the hearts of crash crews nationwide. To wit: The left engine on shutdown exuded great clouds of grayish smoke for about thirty seconds as the engine wound down.

"Not to worry, John. It is a peculiarity of that engine and is no problem."

Try telling that to the crash crews in Albuquerque.

Next trip was to see U-shaped Johnny Long, who was about to be plastered in the hospital. He allowed how he'd had the same problem at heavier gross weights but had not done much work in the approach regime with Sparrow missiles and ammo aboard. Hoo boy!

Several days and some misgivings later, I departed in F7U-3M BuNo. 129736 for San Diego with a fueling stop at El Paso International, where the Vought reps would greet me and service the airplane. The trip was not without its headaches.

I received clearance from the tower to land in El Paso, made a sterling, if speedy approach, and a stellar landing. I taxied behind the follow-me jeep to a VIP location by the operations building and was greeted by three jeeps full of uniformed men with machine guns; the lead jeep was commanded by a guy with eagles on his collar and a .45 on his hip.

In order to ascertain the reasons for the nice welcome, I shut down the machine and you can imagine what the clouds of smoke emanating from the left engine did to stimulate the crash crew. With much arm waving, I persuaded them not to fill the engine with foam, but then the Colonel wanted to know who I was and what the hell I was doing there. It was then the thought crossed my mind that there might be another airfield nearby. I wondered where the Vought guys were.

In the ops building I explained to yet another Colonel that I was Lt. John Moore, USN, flying a highly instrumented new Navy fighter to San Diego and that I could not understand why his command had not received my clearance. I wisely did not ask what was with all the B-47s and -52s parked around.

It was apparent that being an uninvited Navy Lieutenant on a Strategic Air Command base made one less than welcome. But finally, the Vought gang came up from El Paso International Airport ten miles to the south where they had been waiting for me, talked their way through the gates, serviced the machine, and off I went westward, hopefully leaving the SAC personnel with the thought that maybe they had just seen the Navy's first stealth fighter, what with no tail and all. Later, I arrived safely at Miramar.

After some field carrier landing practice at Miramar and further evaluation of the thrust problem, I learned that in an approach turn, the bottom of the thrust-versus-airspeed curve was about 155 knots at these weights and the backside of the curve was Mt. Everest-like, quickly exceeding whatever thrust was being generated at MRT. Landing Signal Officers, of course, are not fond of those abnormally high approach speeds. But ever onward.

To assure the beginning of the tests and to eliminate me from the decision-making loop, -3M No. 736 was hoisted aboard *Shangri-La* at North Island, and I had the ship all to myself for three days of carrier trials with this wondrous machine. Almost every approach required afterburner to stay aloft at gross weights of 25,000 to 26,000 pounds with all ammo and missiles aboard. I became fairly adept at cycling in and out of just the left engine afterburner instead of both to sustain an acceptable approach speed, but there was little question in this pilot's mind that you could never send this airplane to the fleet under these circumstances. Fleet pilots deserved better, besides the fact that such performance would surely take a heavy toll in men and machines.

And so it was in June of '55 that the F7U-3M and I arrived back at Pax River after stops at Miramar, Albuquerque, Dallas, and Marietta. I avoided El Paso.

My debriefing with our Skipper, Bob Calland, attracted a crowd of disbelievers, even drawing Tom Gallagher from the Flying Qualities Branch, whose pilots had not done any field carrier landing practice in the -3M at the heavier gross weights. Calland promptly got into No. 736 for the familiarization and field carrier landing practice and, after one flight, vowed he would never fly it again. But he did, enough to be convinced the -3M could not go to the fleet where pilots would be required to return aboard ship full-up with Sparrows and ammo, as required by BuAer, or BuWeps, or whatever it was called then. Gallagher and J. Lynn Helms each drove the plane under these circumstances and our opinions were coterminous. For sure, the Bureau troops needed opinions from more than a lowly Lieutenant, and they were about to get them.

The Bureau-crats were unified at being horrified: they had ordered ninety-eight of these mothers and were being told they could not go aboard ship. Chance Vought was horrified that the Bureau was horrified. The world's largest conference outside of the United Nations was thereby convened at Flight Test, Pax Riv, with ever-smooth Duke Windsor deftly moderating this menagerie.

Under the Bureau premise that "we have to find a way," discussions finally focused on the new mirror landing system that no U.S. carrier had at that time. The hypothesis was that the thrust would not be so critical in a descending approach as was provided by the mirror. As luck would have it, I was to press onward. The Bureau would provide a fixed mirror landing system in a few weeks, mounted on a forklift, and we would try that. Meanwhile, John Shepherd in one afternoon developed and manufactured his POMOLAS (Poor Man's Optical Landing Aid System), made of painted cardboard pieces mounted on stakes in the ground alongside runway 3l at Pax, set to give a glideslope in the manner of the mirror system. It worked surprisingly well until it got rained on and warped, but it lasted long enough for us to determine that the gliding approach was somewhat of an improvement but still allowed the -3M pilot to get on the backside of the curve at heavy approach weights which required afterburner for survival.

Soon the mirror arrived mounted on its forklift, and it was similar to Shepherd's POMOLAS if brighter and warp-proof. Unfortunately, the Bureau folks latched onto my feeling that there was some improvement (less hairy) and dispatched the forklift, mirror system, the -3M and me back to San Diego and *Shangri-La* for further evaluation of this potential. There was complete unison in San Diego – the *Shangri-La* crew did not want me there and I did not want to be there.

As it turned out, the mirror-on-the-forklift was of little use on the pitching deck given to us by the Pacific Ocean. In two days, I made twenty-five approaches and landings in the -3M including fifteen touch-and-goes and ten traps, using the mirror as a glide-slope starting point, since with the deck going up and down, the mirror might as well have been in the wardroom. Results were about the same as with Shepherd's POMOLAS, in that one could sustain an acceptable approach speed at about MRT, but if you got a little slow, you were on the back of the curve and into afterburner. At the lighter weights, however, with no Sparrows, no ammo, low fuel state, it really was quite pleasant.

The trip back to Pax was not uneventful. I filed for Albuquerque and was catapulted from *Shangri-La* for the voyage to Albuquerque, which was

nominal for a short while. Cruising along at 25,000 feet, I was busy comput-
ing the time at which the -3M and I would penetrate the ADIZ, a Defense
Department control zone which could not be entered without clearance, with
the further requirement that penetration must be within plus or minus ten
minutes from filed estimates. My attention to this matter was distracted by
the distinct feeling that we were flying sideways. A glance at the utility system hydraulic pressure gauge showed zero. The first clue, of course, was the
yawing, since the yaw damper system now had retired. Final calculations
showed I would enter ADIZ as filed, so I set my mind to the unsavory task of
evaluating the condition of No. 736 with zero hydraulic pressure. It was un-
settling to contemplate.

It was mandatory to have the slats out for landing – hydraulic. It
was mandatory to have the gear down – hydraulic. (No slats-in or wheels-
up landings in the F7U!) Nosewheel steering – important – hydraulic. Brakes
– hydraulic. Canopy – hydraulic. Not knowing where the hydraulic fluid
had gone or what was going to happen next, I decided to do something electronic. I switched IFF (Identification, Friend or Foe) from squawk one to
emergency, then advised the world I was about to crash. All this did was
attract some Air Force bastard in an F-86 who came alongside, got all the
dope he needed, wrote me up for missing my ADIZ estimate by two minutes, waved goodbye, and flew away.

The trip into Albuquerque was not comfortable. Advising approach
control of my proclaimed emergency, I requested lots of fire trucks and
meatwagons, remembering Johnny Long bent backwards like a pretzel after
he had run off the runway at Dallas.

Approaching at 10,000 feet and about 200 knots, I made some decisions. I was not going to land that mother with the canopy closed, or the
slats in, or the wheels up. First the canopy. I moved the lever to open and,
sure enough, it unlocked and with the help of the breeze, I was able to push
it fully open. Whether it would stay open in event of a crash was another
matter. But, one down. Next, I selected the slats out – nothing. Actuation of
the emergency air bottle blew them out and locked. Two down. Then I put
the landing gear handle down – nothing. Actuating the emergency gear air
bottle blew the gear down and locked. Three for three!

I was truly worried about being able to keep the -3M on the runway,
with no nosewheel steering and "iffy" brakes. I was aware that without hy-

draulic pressure, there still should be three or four brake applications from the brake reservoir bladder, and there was the emergency brake air bottle as a last resort.

The touchdown at about 125 knots (must have been 135 knots or so at Albuquerque) was smooth, and I busily got the nose over and did a lot of steering with rudders as we decelerated. At near 70 knots, I'd guess, I lost rudder effectiveness and started drifting off the runway to the left. Time for the first brake application. Nothing. No brakes. Heading off the runway, I actuated the emergency brake air bottle. Immediately, the right tire blew as the right wheel locked, but nothing on the left brake. The -3M and I started into a wild skid to the right (thank God, to the right), the airplane rotating clockwise as it skidded down and across the runway, coming to a stop on the right edge facing the direction from which we had approached. Shutting down the engines again caused grave consternation with the alert crash crews who really did not understand Cutlasses or smoke pouring therefrom, but I persuaded them not to flood the port engine with foam, though frankly, my dear, I didn't give a damn at that point.

It turned out that during the cat shot from *Shangri-La*, the catapult bridle had bounced up into the left main gear brake assembly, destroying it and mangling hydraulic lines there in the process. Bad day at Black Rock.

A few days later, after the Voughters had flown in needed parts, the -3M was ready to fly again. So back to Pax River via St. Louis and a new round of talks with the Bureau folks and their ninety-eight F7U-3Ms that we said they couldn't fly aboard ship. They were inclined not to take no for an answer.

Whilst the Bureau, Board of Inspection and Survey, Naval Air Test Center and other muck-a-mucks ranker than this Lieutenant tried to resolve the -3M puzzle, there was other work to be done involving "my" machine: namely, using its mass and instrumentation to help calibrate the newly installed constant-runout arresting gear in place on Pax's runway 31.

On a bright summer morning two of us, an A3D with Bud Nance driving and my -3M, taxied out for some arrested landings in the new gear as part of the evaluation process. It was to be 736's last flight.

I was first, scheduled to arrest as close to ninety-five knots as possible, with No. 736 weighing in at 26,000 pounds. I concluded I would have better speed control if I taxied in rather than flew in, since there was a ten-to-fifteen knot, thirty-degree crosswind and all I had was the airspeed indicator as a measure. John Shepherd and Jerry Vaverek were the masterminds on hand as we were to evaluate a new arresting gear metering valve during runout following arrestment. The LSO, Sam Thompson, stood majestically by his jeep as LSOs do, and at 0700 I started my run from the end of runway 31.

I reached about 103 knots indicated, hopefully the ninety-five knot engaging speed (actual speed proved to be ninety-eight knots), and just before reaching the wire I throttled back, turned on the instrumentation and dropped the hook. Cameras ground, oscillographs whirred, and the hook snagged the arresting cable. Though things happened pretty fast for the next few minutes, I do recall many of the events that followed hook engagement. First, it was apparent to me that I was not slowing down very much – it seemed that the new metering valve was not metering – then suddenly there was a terrific impact.

The arresting cable, a two-inch behemoth, had fully paid out and was two-blocked. The Cutlass, still traveling at an estimated seventy-five knots, was stopped within less than thirty feet by the stretch of the cable alone! The impact failed the nose gear strut, ramming it up through the fuselage just behind the seat, and the Cutlass nose section slammed onto the concrete, fracturing the fuselage almost in two. The ejection seat firing mechanism was actuated, went to a top dead-center pre-fire position, and stopped. Though my shoulder straps were tight, I was propelled forward and downward so hard as to smash my face on the top of the control stick (good old oxygen mask). The deceleration was so profound that, though my hand was on the power control levers at idle, my hand shot forward, putting both engines into afterburner and bending the power control levers all to hell. It was about to get messy.

I was dazed by the blow to the mouth, which loosened teeth and cut lips, but was quickly aware that the Cutlass was still moving, backward, and a sizeable fire had started below the cockpit. The recoil from the stretched arresting cable had pulled the -3M backwards and rotated it ninety degrees to the left. Unfortunately, the hook had released the wire, and the Cutlass, in afterburner, started across the runway toward the weeds.

Pilot reaction was instinctive: I pulled the bent power control levers back, but they were no longer connected to anything. Full afterburner. Depressing the brake pedals produced nothing – they were also sheared. The airplane was accelerating and the fire was roaring. Oh, yes, the emergency brake air bottle, duly actuated, was no longer connected.

As the Cutlass left the runway, accelerating, I realized I could not stay in the cockpit because the fire was engulfing it from below. The escape route was arduous at best. The main gear were at least eight feet out from each side of the cockpit, yet I had no choice I could think of but to dive out of the airplane, now doing about thirty knots, and try to roll clear of the main gear. I unbuckled, stood on the edge of the cockpit, right side, and dived as hard as I could at a forty-five degree angle away from the angry machine, hitting the ground rolling, rolling, rolling. Though I did not see the Cutlass pass over me, I found my seat pack and knee board inside the right main tire track and me on the outside of it, scraped and bloody, but intact.

Standing in the weeds, I saw the Cutlass, sliding on its nose in a ball of fire, slowing to a halt because of an encounter with rough terrain. The cockpit was now completely engulfed in flames and the engines still roaring away in afterburner. No one had seen me get out!

As the fire trucks and a meatwagon raced across the field to the crash site, I walked out of the weeds, across the runway to the LSO jeep where Sam was busy shouting instructions into the radio mike to anyone who would listen.

Thompson looked up as I stood there looking like I had been run over by something, but hadn't, and said, "What in the hell are you doing here?"

I wondered where he thought I should be!

Meanwhile, the fire trucks were pouring foam into the cockpit in hopes of saving enough of the pilot for an open-casket burial, at the same time pouring foam into the intakes of both engines in an effort to flame them out. In moments, the engines were quiet and the fire was out, and from the LSO jeep we watched John Shepherd and Jerry Vaverek, along with the corpsmen, peer into the cockpit in astonishment. There was nobody home! Vaverek thought I had been completely incinerated and Shepherd figured there had to be a body somewhere. There was – at the LSO jeep.

Thompson finally got word to the meatwagon, which raced over, picked me up, and made its way to the Pax hospital. It was now 0715. At this point, I really was not sure I would survive the Cutlass. At sick bay, it took the flight surgeon only a few minutes to determine I would live, wherewith he produced two mini-bottles of brandy with instructions to consume the stuff immediately. I generally did not drink brandy at that hour, but you have to listen to your doctor. Shortly thereafter, as the x-ray machine was touring my back, another flight surgeon came in, took one look and said to the corpsman, "Get that son-of-a-bitch some brandy." Eight ounces later, I was smashed. It was now 0800.

Other than a bunch of loose teeth, a sore mouth, lots of scrapes and bruises and a hangover, I was fine. F7U-3M No. 736 was fatally injured. Johnny Long's -3M, with mine, made it two down and ninety-six to go.

Unfortunately, BuAer, or whoever, provided carrier suitability with yet another F7U-3M – good old BuNo. 139868. In the next few months, I had the privilege of flying 868 off three more carriers trying to convince the buyer that the -3M Cutlass never should be flown off aircraft carriers. Well, off maybe, but not onto! The Bureau folks, logically, asked that we define an acceptable gross weight at which the airplane could be flown safely onto carriers by fleet units, since they would soon be up to their asses in F7Us. There probably was none, but I seem to remember that we stipulated 23,000 pounds max, where there was a small margin of error thrust-wise, but which meant to BuAer a lot of weight reduction in armament and the like, since empty (fuel) gross weight with Sparrows was more than 23,000 pounds.

Anyway, I did not participate in the final decision-making process, having, for my valiant efforts, been assigned as the USS Yorktown's (CVA-10) handling officer.

Not long after, on a clear day somewhere in the Pacific, the Yorktown was joined by another carrier sporting a squadron of F7U-3Ms. During our first day of joint operations, I watched from my perch under an AD-6 on the flight deck as the -3M was catapulted from our sister carrier. Immediately after becoming airborne, long streaks of flame came pouring out of the starboard engine as the pilot tried to gain some altitude. Sadly, at less than 1,000 feet, the Cutlass nosed over, trailing black smoke, and splashed into the blue water, taking its pilot with it.

Shortly afterward, that squadron was offloaded at Atsugi and spent its WestPac tour with the pilots flying Combat Air Patrol over Mt. Fuji during the day while chasing sashimi with Asahi beru at night.

On this and the next page a crash sequence aboard *Essex:*

Above: A landing McDonnell F2H-1 Banshee (center foreground) overshoots the arresting gear and speeds toward parked aircraft. The author is just exiting the nearest parked Banshee, to the right, just behind the scurrying deck crew.

Below: The runaway fighter is just crashing into the parked planes and John Moore is only partially out of his cockpit.

Above: The inevitable explosion occurs, John Moore's aircraft is enveloped in flames and he is flung overboard.

Below: Flames engulf the *Essex* 's deck, starboard forward gun bays and burn on the water alongside where the author fights for survival with other victims.

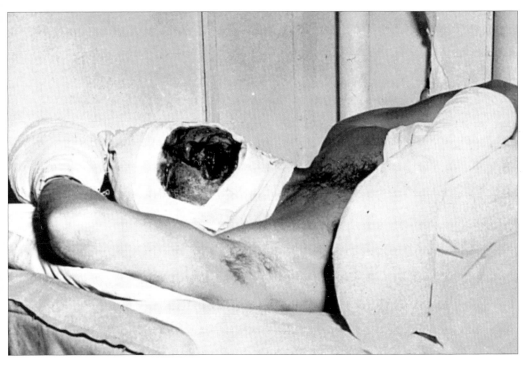

John Moore in sick bay on *Essex* after his rescue.

En route home, John Moore displays his burned hands.

The three surviving pilots from the *Essex* fire, (l. to r.) Sluis, Bauer, and Moore, at Yokosuka Naval Hospital, Japan.

On this and the next page is a crash sequence at Pax River NAS. Above, John Moore has just landed the F7U-3M Cutlass and speeds by the camera at a speed of nearly 100 knots.

The nose gear of the Cutlass collapses and the plane is immediately out of control.

Veering off the runway, the Cutlass breaks just aft of the cockpit as the first fire begins to flare.

John Moore got out just before fire engulfed the entire nose section.

The aircraft, drenched in retardant foam.

The wreckage is hoisted for removal, displaying the full extent of the fire.

Naval Aviation Cadet John Moore in an N3N biplane trainer, 1943.

Ensign John Moore on graduation at
Corpus Christi NAS, 1 Dec 1944.

John Moore with his first Grumman
F6F-3 Hellcat, 1945.

Above: Grumman F8F-1 Bearcats landing aboard the carrier, *Philippine Sea.* The near aircraft has just arrested as another rolls into the groove. The Landing Signal Officer's paddles can just be seen above the screen in his roost on the port stern corner.

Below: LSO, Lcdr. Harry Dobbs, doing his job bringing home the *Philippine Sea's* aircraft.

World War II hero, ace
Stanley "Swede" Vejtasa,
who retired as captain.

Lt. Kirk Hershey comes aboard
Philippine Sea from a destroyer that
rescued him after he ditched his
Bearcat in the Mediterranean.

John Moore on wing of a Bearcat, dressed for high altitude flight at NAS Charleston, RI in 1947

The Cutlass took too many lives before it was retired. Wrong stuff. It was anathema. Yet, as maturity sculptures the mind, one tends to remember the good things, the happy things, and forget the unpleasant ones. So it is with most of us who survived the Cutlass. We remember it as fun to fly.

But would I do it again? Are you kidding? Of course!

III

BUT IN THE BEGINNING

The Short Arm Inspection. That is really the only test WW II fledgling aviators remember about the exams they took in hopes of becoming Aviation Cadets. Oh, we took academic exams, were interviewed by psychologists of sorts, and had complete physicals, but in the memory bank, all pales compared to recollections of our first short arm inspection. It was embarrassing and dehumanizing for most eighteen-year-old young men in those days, many being virgins and sexually experienced only through fantasies of seducing one movie starlet or another.

The short arm inspection was a rather rudimentary test to determine if an individual had some unseemly creatures harbored in his reproductive equipment, a circumstance looked upon unfavorably by the United States Navy and other services recruiting aviation cadets.

In December of 1942, twenty of us, all about eighteen years of manhood, were taking a battery of exams at a Navy facility in St. Louis, hoping to be accepted as Naval Aviation Cadets and ultimately to wear the Navy Wings of Gold.

On this memorable day, we had completed most tests and were ready for the final physical exam, during which we were totally undressed for several inspections including potential hemorrhoids and the ultimate exam. Not one of us was embarrassed by the nudity, having grown up in YMCA and summer camp environments, so this was routine, sort of. We were marched single file into a large examination room toward a table, behind which sat two Navy medical corpsmen, the inspectors. In front of me was a big, happy-go-lucky country boy full of energy and enthusiasm and having the time of his life. However, an unwanted transformation began in his sexual parts, continuing until his equipment was sizable and pointing northward. He was a bit uneasy about the event but just laughed about it. I was embarrassed for him and all eyes were on this natural phenomenon as Country Boy approached the exam table.

The others ahead of him had been instructed to "milk her down," which meant for us to squeeze the male part as the corpsmen watched for signs of any bad things which might indicate trouble within. As Country Boy arrived at the table with his equipment absolutely ready for the reproduction process, one of the corpsmen took out a small hammer, the kind doctors use to check arm and leg reflexes, and rapped this very firm protrusion on its head. Country Boy winced, as did we all, at the sight of this happening, but all it seemed to do was make this thing angry and it stood there more resolute than ever. So the corpsman whacked it again, which, amazingly enough, it seemed to enjoy; wherewith the corpsman ordered Country Boy back to the locker room where he was told to stay until this weapon was disarmed.

Unfortunately, there were two doors out of the examination room, one to the locker room and the other to the office area and, as luck would have it, Country Boy opened the wrong door and took his weapon into a room full of secretaries. Their shrieks told everyone on the ten th floor that something was amiss. Of course, Country Boy made a hasty retreat back into the exam room then into the locker room, followed by a medium-size but formidable lieutenant commander. We could hear through the door (hatch) that Country Boy was being advised in clear terms to get his clothes on and get the hell out of there and never come back.

The poor guy had washed out before he ever got in. We all were sorry for him but felt he would do just fine in the Marines. When the dust settled and short arm inspections were completed we found that one lad had been friendly with a naughty girl and was soiled. He was sent home to see a doctor.

At the end of the exam routines, Naval Aviation accepted and signed up twelve of us on the spot. Aviation Cadets yet! For me, it was the beginning of a life-long career as an airplane driver.

We never saw Country Boy again. Though the Navy thought he had the wrong stuff, I expect a lot of young maidens in Iowa believed otherwise.

The Navy wanted me to complete my third year at the Missouri School of Mines in Rolla before calling me to active duty and into flight training, designated the V-5 program. And so in July of 1943, I became a real live

Naval Aviation Cadet enroute to becoming a fighter pilot, hopefully, with further aspirations of single-handedly winning the war in the Pacific for the U.S. and A. For one with such lofty goals, the beginning was inauspicious. It seemed that before I was to face the enemy, I had to learn how to make a bed, march with a rifle, do a right flank harch, and wrestle some bastard twice my size in PT. It was Prep-Flight School at Murray State College, Murray, Kentucky. No cockpits there.

In early July, a group of us new Aviation Cadets had mustered in St. Louis for a train ride to Murray. All in civilian clothes, we were offloaded at the station, bussed to the college campus and offloaded again into the presence of our platoon officer, a tubby little Ensign with the voice of a raptor. In the following eight weeks, we were properly uniformed, we learned to march, salute, say "aye, aye, sir," and we were exposed to sufficient academics to weed out the mentally deficient, which was about twenty percent of our crop. After eight weeks, those who had not learned to swim were out. It seemed the Navy operated mostly on the water, and if our ship sank we would just swim 800 miles to Guam.

Our platoon officer, Ensign Tub-O-Lard, was irascible as platoon leaders are supposed to be. As best we could tell, El Tub-O had never seen a ship, or an ocean for that matter. He was fresh out of South Dakota where they are a little short of oceans. His specialty was hospital corners. He was an expert in making beds and daily inspections of our rooms invariably revealed deficiencies in our bunk-making prowess. In retrospect, we did rather quickly learn hospital corners through the medium of marching with a rifle for two hours after the evening meal for every faulty corner. It gave one ample time to reflect on Ensign Tub-O's teachings. It was an instructional tool used throughout our flight training program with considerable success. As we left Prep Flight School for flight training, actually flying real live airplanes, we left behind twenty-five percent of our group who, as far as Naval aviation was concerned, had the wrong stuff!

Those of us who survived Prep Flight School were dispatched to various flying facilities about the country where we might learn to fly. I was sent, by train of course, to Davenport, Iowa, for what the Navy called WTS, War Training Service. Some ten of my buddies made that trek, including my newfound friend Rick Williams.

In Davenport, we were escorted to the St. Ambrose College campus, where we would be harbored until we either learned to fly or were washed out. The most surprising aspect of the welcome was that the Navy personnel seemed to want us there, as opposed to the atmosphere at Prep Flight School where we were tolerated at best and seemingly not wanted at worst.

Rick and I were roommates at St. Ambrose and shared an extraordinary desire to fly airplanes. Neat guy, Rick. We studied our ground school lessons together, competed amiably in phys-ed, and were totally ready to fly off the grass field airport in Davenport, which housed a cadre of small Aeronca flight trainers, tandem-seating-tail-draggers that were magnificent to us.

My flight instructor was Mr. Bill Wade, a crusty, forty-five year old, very patient man. My first flight with him was elegant beyond description. We were programmed to solo after eight hours of dual instruction, and what an incredible thrill it was when my instructor climbed out of the airplane and told me to make three take-offs and landings all by my lonesome. Every aviator, male or female, vividly remembers his or her first solo. I had 8.1 hours of flight time when I found that I was airborne all by myself. An extraordinary experience. Rick soloed the same day and we celebrated for hours after the evening meal with cokes and cookies in the small lounge downstairs in our dorm.

Surprising what is remembered after such an event. We had a nickelodeon in our lounge with some new offerings available. Rick inserted five cents from his seventy-five-dollar-a-month salary and played a song from a group no one had ever heard of – The Mills Brothers. The song? "Paper Doll." I play that recording to this day, fifty years later.

The following day was full of promise. I made my second solo and awaited Rick who was still airborne solo in his Aeronca. We had learned so many things about flying in such a short time. Watch your airspeed, check for traffic around you, don't stretch a glide, use carb heat, don't stretch a glide. As seasoned pilots know, you can't stretch a glide – meaning that if you get slow in your final approach you must add power to maintain flying speed.

Rick was wide and long in his approach and entered a longer than normal straightaway. We watched as he glided at idle power, carb heat on, toward the grass runway. He was low. Add power, Rick. The nose of his trainer got higher and higher. Add power, Rick. RICK – ADD POWER!

About 200 yards from the fence, the plane stalled, nosed over and slammed into the ground as a mass of crumpled metal, then flipped over. We ran toward the wreckage but were stopped by two flight instructors who did not want us to see anymore. Rick was dead.

It was the first of too many memorial services I attended in my years as an airplane driver. This was the precursor of all the others – green pastures, sitting at the right hand, the glory of death. Bull shit! There was no glory in Rick's death. That was not God's will! We have a better God than that, I remember thinking then – and now. Packing Rick's belongings for shipment to his folks was not easy. As time passed and with others it got no easier.

While I was there, our little WTS school acquired an absolutely beautiful N3N biplane open-cockpit trainer. Love at first sight. It mattered not that the outside temperatures were below freezing, the open cockpit airplane with natural air conditioning was Utopian to us "veteran" pilots with almost thirty hours of flight time.

Meanwhile, a social event was arranged with a group of student nurses in training nearby. We Cadets were bussed to a party fraught with cookies, cokes, and delightful young ladies, backed up with a live five-piece band. Oh, joy.

Though I was not much of a dancer, I was a great holder-tighter. It took little time for me to fall in love with an adorable five-foot blond who danced closer than allowed. As we swayed to the Sammy Kaye type music, my new found love whispered into my ear the most sensual sounds I had heard in eons. She breathed what sounded like "mareseadoatsndoeseadoatsnliddle-lambsydivy." I had no idea what it meant or what language it was, but I knew it was sexual. My things knew it was sexual even before I did and immediately began preparing themselves for any event which might follow.

I asked again what she said in this moment of passion and she said, "You know the song – mareadoats n' stuff" – I didn't. I asked what it meant and she said: "Mares eat oats and does eat oats – it's a song!" In my land-based Naval career that was my first "oh shit." It would not be my last. Sexual parts – cool it.

After three hours of dual in the N3N, I soloed that lovely old bird, even then being replaced by the Stearman biplane trainer. What a thrill. Cold as hell in the open cockpit but pure exhilaration. The weather was unsettled for my fourth N3N solo but no matter.

Returning to the field for landing and in my final approach, I was greeted by my instructor and another standing in the middle of the runway waving frantically at me as if I were landing wheels up, except these wheels were fixed down. I decided not to land in order to avoid killing the two instructors, and as I flew over their heads, I saw to my horror two planes approaching from the opposite direction for landing.

I had taken off to the south but the wind had shifted, the barn-size wind tee had been reversed, and now all traffic was taking off and landing to the north. All except Johnny Boy. Everybody in Iowa knew of the runway change, but there is always someone who doesn't get the word.

The flight administrative gang was reasonably tolerant, and all I had to do was wash and wax the wind tee every day for a week. It looked quite good toward the end. Radio communications certainly would have helped, but we were not introduced to radios in flying machines until advanced training in Corpus Christi. Meanwhile, don't blink.

In less than two months, I graduated from WTS with forty-five flight hours and all the eagerness of an Eagle Scout. It was on to Pre-Flight School in Iowa City. In the few weeks in Davenport, a lot of good things had happened and some not-so-good. We had lost Rick. Another lad had an engine failure and glided into a too small field, plowed through a fence and a cow, ending up in a stand of unfriendly trees. Both plane and pilot were broken. The pilot lived – the Aeronca trainer did not. That was the young man's last flight in Naval aviation, which took a dim view of people breaking up its airplanes. Wrong stuff.

No one wants to read much about Pre-Flight School. It was a tough eight weeks; combative, disciplined, bloody, intellectual, bloody. But kind of fun. In phys-ed, we boxed until we were bloody, played soccer until we bled (sometimes it seemed without a soccer ball), wrestled, played basketball, judo – bleed, men, bleed. Ever see a bloody nose in badminton? Pre-Flight School, Iowa, winter, '43.

In academics, we took celestial navigation until we literally saw stars. We stood in the freezing air at night sighting the Big Dipper, Orion, Polaris, et al. Our instructor pointed out the small constellation, the Seven Sisters, but when we could only see six of them, he explained that one of them was not very bright [Lieutenant (j.g.) joke]. I never used celestial nav after leaving Pre-Flight. We learned to receive Morse Code at sixteen words a minute.

In my flying career, I never used more than five letters: A (dit da), N (da dit), used in radio navigation in instrument training, and of course, S.O.S. (dit dit dit, da da da, dit dit dit), the international emergency call letters, but also an item served too frequently at breakfast (creamed chip beef on toast, i. e., "stuff" on a shingle).

It was at Pre-Flight, however, that I learned the Navy had a heart. For all its discipline and militarism, there is a softness within. I started out as a Company Commander because I was the loudest and ended up as Cadet Regimental Commander because I was the tallest. It was in this phase of my glory that the stuff hit the fan.

One of my three roommates brought home a goldfish one day, named Goldie, naturally. We kept her in our wash basin at night and surreptitiously stashed in a tall water glass in the medicine cabinet during the day when routine room inspections might prove fatal to her.

Toward the very end of our tour in Iowa City, the roommate who had the goldfish storing duty forgot to transfer Goldie to the medicine cabinet. Bad news. The four of us were called out of class for an on-the-double trek to the Battalion Commander's office. This gentleman, a three-striper, was twice as broad as Mike Tyson and meaner. He could not believe that we could insult "his" Navy by floating a goldfish in "his" wash basin. I mean — MEAN! That was one pissed-off officer and as the four of us stood in front of Commander Thick-Neck, we were sure our flying days were over. All about a goldfish? Finally, we were dismissed before any seepage of urine was detected on the floor, and as we marched out of the office a voice bellowed, "Moore, wait one!"

I turned around and waited one. The Commander said softly, "Goldie is in good hands. My daughter is taking care of her. She'll be just fine."

"Thank you, sir!" sez I, then got the hell out of there. The Navy had a heart!

"E" as in Elimination; Olathe, Kansas, in late winter '43 was elimination base. Flying the Stearman biplane trainer, a surprising number of which still grace the skies over our country this day in 1995, was a dream come true. What a toy for a twenty-year-old kid. A dream come true, indeed.

I have many memories of Olathe, some of which I would like to share. The first event taught me a lesson life-time retained. First day, first things first: Establish who would lead the Cadet Corps at Olathe. That was easy, since I was Cadet Regimental Commander at Pre-Flight – who else? We Cadets were cordoned into company-size groups, two platoons per company, and as specific names were called by the Naval officers running the show, each named individual had the opportunity to march a platoon for a few minutes to show leadership skills. In this phase, my name did not come up. It figured. Then Company Commanders were selected. Still no call for Johnny Boy. They were obviously saving me for the big stick.

The Cadet Regimental Commander was chosen and it was not I. How could this be? Big hero at Pre-Flight? I didn't even make squad leader because some sombich was taller than I.

What I learned there at Olathe was that it is not what you have been, but what you are and can be that matters. Most people and organizations care little about what you have been but more about your potential and what you can do for them. Don't rest on your laurels, or on your ass, or you will spend a lot of time sitting on it. I learned. Maybe it was the goldfish.

The next thing that happened was traumatizing. I had been at E base for almost two weeks, had soloed the Stearman, and was already into acrobatics. I kept thinking, "Are they really paying me for this?" (seventy-five dollars a month). Then a call came to the barracks one afternoon which advised me that an Ensign Morris Sievert was at the main gate to see me. Impossible.

My best friend in college (and still today fifty-three years later) was a guy named Sievert. From him I learned to be a follower. He was president of the sophomore class; I was vice-president. He was president of the junior class; I was v.p. Then I went off to fight the war while he finished up at Rolla, Missouri. So it could not be the same Sievert. But it was. I'd been in the Navy for a year, and I am an Aviation Cadet; Sievert had been in the Navy for fifteen minutes, and he is an Ensign!

Well, Sievert and I had a great visit, he insisting on my saluting him with nauseating frequency. He told me that he was on the way to the Pacific as Exec of a 200-foot amphibious vessel designated an LSM, which stood for Landing Ship Mediocre as best I could tell. And so Sievert and his LSM and hundreds of others steamed their way across the Pacific Ocean at six knots.

Subsequently, I made six trips across the Pacific on aircraft carriers and that is a BIG ocean. If you are going to do it at six knots, you'd better take a lunch – a big lunch.

Anyway, whilst I am in flight training, Sievert's LSM supported the Saipan and Okinawa operations, and he became a big hero at Okinawa. Sievert and his ship could generate enough smoke to obscure half the Pacific fleet from Kamikaze attacks and that was without using his smoke generators. That's just the way he ran his engine room. So my friend Sievert ended up with more medals than McArthur and I was still in flight training. Every time I see him these days he reminds me.

In an air filled with motivated Cadets came a camaraderie extraordinaire among many of us. My buddy was P. J. Patrick ("Pat," of course) who bunked above me in our barracks, which housed more than fifty Cadets. Pat was delightful to be around. His girlfriend and fiance´, all of eighteen and living in nearby Kansas City, visited Pat every weekend. She was adorable and became my fantasy during sleepy hours as I swept her away in my arms and carried her to a life filled with love. I did not mention this to Pat or Anne. Clear thinking, John.

As we learned acrobatics in the Stearman´, we were assigned many solo hours to practice loops, snap rolls, figure eights – the gambit. Whenever Pat and I were scheduled off at the same time, we would meet over a given field and show off to one another, each in his own Stearman. I would do a loop as Pat watched from some 500 feet away; then he would do a loop. I'd do a snap roll: he'd do a snap roll. His were better than mine. So I am thinking I'll show this sombich some real flying. I rolled inverted and just hung by the seat belt and shoulder straps (I never liked that) until the engine quit, then rolled upright as the engine started up rather quickly. Okay, Pat, your turn.

Pat rolled inverted and in seconds fell out of his airplane. Unbelievable! I saw him falling below as the Stearman righted itself and headed on a downward spiral toward the ground. After much too long an interval, I saw a 'chute pop open probably about 2,000 feet above the ground, and I dived down to circle Pat as he crunched into a farmer's field and his 'chute collapsed. His Stearman plowed into the ground several hundred yards from Pat but did not burn. They usually do.

I circled Pat and he indicated he was okay, so I roared off to NAS Olathe to report the event. At the ops building there was some excitement and a lieutenant (j.g.) instructor ordered me to accompany him in another Stearman to the crash site, which I did, of course. Meanwhile, the farmer whose land now housed a crumpled Stearman and a sensitized Cadet, tractored out, picked up Pat and took him to his farmhouse. A phone call to the NAS announced that farmer Whoever had Pat and was bringing him to the air base. Never mind what the Captain said, farmer Whoever was not waitin' for no dagnab ambulance and was branging this boy in hisself. The least he could do for his country. And what is a Captain anyway?

I led the duty j.g. to the bent Stearman but there was not much to see. Bent metal. He circled the crash several times as was befitting a lieutenant (j.g.), then raced home at 90 mph to report the five acres of destroyed soybeans which farmers usually reported to the government in such a happening.

Pat and Anne were devastated. His future in Naval aviation was clearly in doubt. Interestingly enough on his behalf, the accident investigation team found a suspect seat belt in the wreckage, which most likely was the cause of Pat's mishap. After a week of suspense he was flying again, exonerated of any blame. Happy days – back in the air again.

I lost track of Pat after "E" base when we moved en masse to advanced training at Corpus Christi along with many others who were funneled in from other "E" bases. I learned, however, that Pat and Anne did not marry. Pat did not get his Wings of Gold. He was killed in a mid-air collision over Corpus Christi two weeks before he was to be commissioned Ensign, U.S. Navy.

We were introduced to formation flying, which was a blast. Usually, we flew in three-plane formations with gentle turns and climbs and finally with formation take-offs and landings. Incrediboble, as Pogo would say.

One day, three of us were practicing our formation exercises followed by an instructor monitoring as a loose fourth in his Stearman. Part of the exercise was to do touch-and-go landings in formation at an outlying grass field with ample runways for the events. I was flying number two wing, left side, on our leader whose name does not appear in my log, and Harry Crawford was flying number three, right side, stepped down as I was.

Our first formation touch-and-go was perfect. From the corner of my eye, I saw our instructor flying with us as we took off for a second landing. In these exercises, all eyes are glued on the leader. If he screws up, we is in deep yogurt as they say. On our second landing, it seemed to me we were rather far down the strip before we touched down in formation and when we added power to follow the lead plane on take off, I observed from a quick glance that our instructor pilot was staying on the ground. Le clue.

As we took off, I thought I saw a formidable stand of trees menacing ahead. Just before the forest became a factor, I glanced up again and saw that I was not going to clear the branches. I immediately pulled up and away to the left, then looked back to see that our glorious leader had barely cleared the trees but Harry had not.

Harry's plane struck the tree trunks and branches, which dragged it to the ground where it cartwheeled, shedding its wings in an ominous cloud of dust. I saw our instructor shut down his plane and start running toward the crash site. He waved once at our two remaining planes, and as best I could tell was pointing toward NAS Olathe. No helicopters in those days. No radios, no crash trucks, no communications, no meatwagons on site.

I immediately departed the scene for Olathe as Cadet So-and-So circled the field for whatever reason. In those days, the Stearman had an external cranking mechanism used to start the engine. Two sailors would crank their asses off winding a spring device then clear out of the way as the pilot engaged the starter. So the instructor trying to help Harry at the crash site would be there until someone showed up with a crank. All the more reason for me to get back to the air station as fast as possible for help.

By the time I landed, help was on its way thanks to someone passing by who saw the crash and phoned in the news. Not knowing this, I ran into the ops building out of breath and was greeted by a surly ensign who said, "Not you again!" Bearer of bad tidings strikes again.

Harry was torn up but lived. The Stearman died. Cadet So-and-So appeared before a review board, which was not impressed with his judgement, and he was invited to become an ex-Aviation Cadet forthwith. Wrong stuff.

In early spring of '44, I climbed onto a train full of Cadets headed for advanced training, Corpus Christi, Texas. E Base had been a wonderful, challenging experience. We approached Corpus with confidence and determination. Could our Wings of Gold be far away? The answer was "YES."

All the WW II Navy Avcads will recall the iterations of advanced flight training – flying the great old Vultee BT-13 Vibrator at Cabanis Field, on to instruments at Beeville, then the final enchilada in North American SNJ Texans at Kingsville. At the end of Kingsville there was a Navy blue uniform with Wings of Gold and an Ensign stripe on each sleeve – cost was one month's pay, seventy-five dollars. I still have my original Naval officer's blue uniform – now with three stripes on it – hanging in the hall closet awaiting my demise and a trip to Arlington. Hang in there blues.

The Vibrator was a fledgling pilot's delight. Fixed gear, flaps, two-speed prop, i.e, high pitch for take-off and low pitch for cruise, and lots of noise.

During our initial ground training days before the BT-13, we were reminded that this was still the Navy and this was unquestionably military. Case in point: There were four of us in a room and each morning at the sound of a recorded version of reveille, we were to leap out of our bunks and stand at attention for a few moments before we were allowed to be normal. When the third morning dawned, reveille sounded and immediately our door (hatch) opened and a round-faced ensign yelled, "On your feet and stand at attention." Three of us leaped out of our bunks; the fourth did not. It seemed that his system was engrossed in a typical nineteen year old's awakening syndrome within his personal parts and he was too embarrassed to get up. The ensign showed zero understanding and ordered that cadet up NOW. The poor bastard lumbered out of his bunk using his pillow to conceal his indiscretion, for which he was privileged to march with a rifle for six hours over three evenings. That would teach that goddam cadet not to wake up with a hard on.

Flying the Vultee Vibrator was just plain fun. One of the events I remember most vividly involved a class of Hispanics, mostly Mexican, which was in training as we were, except their instructors spoke Spanish. We had little intermingling with them because of the language barrier.

In this phase of training, we had radio communications available but that medium was only to be used under exceptional circumstances. For example, all take-off and landing traffic was controlled from the field tower by light – red or green. Take-off and land on green: don't move your ass on red.

One day within the first few weeks I was number two for take-off, solo, behind another solo who turned out to be Hispanic. I watched him get the green light and off he went, but the engine sound was all wrong. He was trying to take-off in low pitch. No way, Jose. He rolled and rolled down the runway without gaining flying speed, finally roaring off the end of the runway in a massive cloud of dirt and dust. Fortunately, there was a lot of tumbleweed and space before the fence and he managed to get stopped and turned around before destroying the fence or the airplane.

From where I sat in my cockpit, it looked like a dust storm down there, enhanced by all the crash trucks, meatwagons and security vehicles pursuing el pilota. Out of the cloud of debris came the airplane, now back on the end of the runway and taxiing toward the center of the field, followed by about six emergency type vehicles.

From the control tower came a strong voice, "Return to the line." Wrong language. When the Hispanic reached the spot from which he started his take-off run, he spun his Vibrator around and radioed, "Ka-bon-is tower, Ka-bon-is tower, I weel try again." Red lights notwithstanding, off he went, still in low pitch. Emergency vehicles scattered as Hispanic roared back down the runway. All the vehicles turned to follow this adventurer from south of the border.

Once again, off the runway in an atomic-size cloud of dust. This time as he emerged back on the runway, he had several vehicles in front of him, one on each side, and one or two behind. On the radio we heard, "Ka-bon-is tower, Ka-bon-is tower, I deed not make eet." Of course, I have no idea what disposition was made of the intrepid young aviator but I expect he made a lot of pesos selling insurance which requires his kind of perseverance.

The Vibrators were fun. I would like to have one nearby today just to touch and smell. But then in 1944, it was on to instruments in Beeville, Texas.

The driving of airplanes from the back seat (SNJs) under a hood on instruments was a lesson in living or dying. What I learned at Beeville was fundamental to my survival when I ended up in night fighters within a year of Beeville at the tender age of twenty-two. Yet what I remember so vividly from Beeville was not so much the "dit das" and "da dits" of an instrument approach, but about Texans.

One of my buddies was "Steve" Quick. Everyone to him was "Steve." Steve Moore. Steve Smith. I do not even remember his first name, but it was not Steve. We had a long weekend for some reason and "Steve" Quick and I decided we would hitchhike to Corpus, some eighty miles away as I remember, to see the new movie *Going My Way* with Bing Crosby.

55

The road to Corpus was long, straight, two-lane and landscaped with tumbleweed and few turn-offs. We were fortunate to be picked up by a gen-u-ine Texan in a pickup truck heading all the way to Corpus. He admired our uniforms and patriotism and was pleased to give us a ride.

Texan expounded ad nauseam about the privilege of living in this God blest land as we rolled along this Godforsaken highway. "Steve" Quick never stopped laughing. He was one happy man. Great smile, lots of teeth, wonderfully outgoing. Then it happened. Texan was saying in his drawl that there was nothing like the freedom of this land – freedom to do anything outdoors. Then he said, "If a man's gotta' pee he can just stop, get out of his car, and pee. That's how it is." "Steve" laughed hard, and said, "That's what I say – piss on Texas!" Wrong!

I watched Texan as "Steve" laughed at his own humor, and Texan got very red, gritted his teeth, then slammed on the brakes and pulled over. "This is as far as I go – get out." There wasn't a side road in sight in either direction. We stepped out in the reddish dirt as Texan raced off toward Corpus Christi, alone.

It was probably an hour that we stood beside the road waiting for another ride to Corpus. A nice family finally picked us up and asked what the hell we were doing out there. "Steve" explained but not very well. However, *Going My Way* was a great movie. We took a bus back to Beeville.

Never say "piss on Texas" to a Texan who is giving you a free ride.

My most memorable flight in this phase of training was an instrument take-off. Under a hood in the back seat of an SNJ, the student was to set his gyro compass when the instructor had positioned the flying machine for take-off, then on command was to take off using only flight gauges. No looky, no peeky. On this occasion, I set my gyro compass on zero and was a ready, confident sombich when told to GO.

Full power and we accelerated down the runway. I kept the gyro compass perfectly on zero as we attained take-off speed. But at this point from under the bottom of the hood my peripheral vision detected grass beneath the SNJ instead of runway. Grass? Wrong. We were airborne, climbing, wings level when the instructor sez, "I got it." Then I realized I had failed to uncage the gyro compass and said, "Sir . . ." Instructor interrupted me and said, "Moore, you would do better if you uncaged your goddam gyro." How'd he know?

"Leave us try it again," sez he. Thank God he had a sense of humor, of sorts. We landed, taxied back to take-off position, when Instructor sez, "Moore, don't screw up again. Are you ready?"

"Yes, sir. Let's go."

I spent the next hour on the gauges and apparently got away with fundamental stupidity through the tolerance of a congenial instructor who laughingly admitted that he was hyper from having spent the previous evening enjoying the treasures of a young maiden, an experience I was yet to know.

We finished instruments, then it was on to Kingsville and the final stages of training before the Wings of Gold. On the first weekend there and before classes started, three of us put on our best, cleanest uniforms and took off for Laredo with a goal of allowing the Mexican people to fawn over us Aviation Cadets as we crossed the border into Nuevo Laredo, Mexico.

The difference between Laredo and Nuevo Laredo was surprising to us: on one side of the river, Americans; and on the other side, Mexicans. Who'd have thought?

We were greeted by an amiable fellow named "Pedro" (he said), who acted as if he had been personally assigned to us for our pleasure by El Presidente himself. Spoke good English, dressed well, looked Mexican. He would devote his day to us and show us his city, Nuevo Loredo. Seemed fair.

After a few hours of looking and shopping with Pedro, he hailed a taxi, invited us to climb aboard and get comfortable. Pedro was taking us to a party. At the end of a short drive over dirt roads to the outskirts of the city, we pulled up in front of a very nice house, nice gardens, some chickens, but generally quite presentable.

Inside we were greeted by a nice Senora, about thirty, who seemed to know Pedro well and who greeted us warmly with some recognizable English. In moments, three pretty girls appeared, about twentyish I guessed, who were also very friendly but who spoke no English. It was only THEN I realized we were in a whorehouse. Surprise!

Each girl latched onto a Cadet. Mine was Rosa, dressed scantily in a yellow wraparound something, and very friendly. Was it possible that the virgin Johnny Boy was about to become an ex-virgin? I knew what you were supposed to do in whorehouses but some questions lingered as to how.

It seemed rather soon after we arrived and were midway through our first beer that the Senora spoke softly to my two compatriots, who were then escorted out of the living room by their girl friends. Senora then advised me that Rosa wanted to take me to her room. Oh, gee!

The door had barely closed behind us when Rosa said, "Cinco dolla, por favor." Even I understood that. The room was equipped with a small dresser, a chair, a pan of water, a towel, and a bed. All the necessities. I laid cinco dolla on the dresser and before it settled, Rosa's wraparound was on the floor and she was nekked right there in front of me.

It took some fumbling before I got my uniform off and draped over a chair. I was surprised and somewhat embarrassed to find my personal things very aware and ready for action. Rosa lay down as I sat on the bed awaiting instructions when she said, "Rubber." I understood that, too. but I told her I did not have a rubber. She said, "Sheet," which I also understood, then quickly got up, put on her wraparound while speaking with agitation in Spanish which I did not understand although I believed it not to be Biblical in nature.

Rosa returned and quickly was nekked again. Then she said "dos hifty mas." Another two hifty? That would be a total of $7.50 I would have invested in this enterprise, which was ten percent of my month's pay. Too late to back out.

With some fumbling, the two of us got this gadget properly placed and she laid down again as I looked with some surprise at her. I had never seen one of those things up close and personal before. Then Rosa pointed down there and said, "Aqui." So much for foreplay.

Some things are instinctive, otherwise there would be no birds or bees or little animals or babies, so with some assistance from Rosa, we consummated this $7.50 transaction, although it seemed to me it was over about the same time it began. Almost before I knew it, I was sitting on the edge of the bed again. Quickly, Rosa removed my mini-raincoat, handed me a towel, put on her yellow wraparound and was gone. I kept thinking, "What happened?"

With uniform once again in place, I walked out into the living room area where Rosa was laughing with Pedro and though I could not understand them, I believe she was explaining to Pedro that an Errol Flynn I wasn't. I also noticed that I was the only Cadet there. In later years, there was a manu facturing logistical term for it: L-I-F-O; last in, first out. My mass-of-muscles Cadet companion was first in, last out, and his girl friend seemed happier than mine – considerably.

When the dust settled, Pedro escorted us back across the border to the Navy pro-station manned by Navy medical corpsmen who were there to prevent the entire Cadet corps from being wiped out by V.D. Pedro extracted cinco dolla from each of us and bid us adios.

It was a fun bus ride back to Kingsville as we bragged about our newly discovered sexual prowess. I kept thinking of that old adage, "How time flies when you are having fun." God did it fly! I also kept thinking that it's got to be better than that. It got better – much better.

Final stages of flight training in the North American SNJ Texan at Kingsville were wonderful and memorable. If all went well, I would get my wings in mid-December, 1944, then be off to F6F Hellcats somewhere. The war needed me.

There was mostly joy, yet some sadness. Mass-of-Muscles of Nuevo Laredo whorehouse fame had played football for some Big Ten team and had a perfect record all the way through training. No downs here. I cannot remember his name nor can I find it in my records. But I remember him.

In the first few weeks of SNJs at Kingsville, we found we were flying mostly solo. Getting time and experience. One afternoon, Mass-of-Muscles was shooting landings at an outlying field and apparently after one take-off as he was climbing out, he reached to pull his prop pitch back, but instead, grabbed his mixture control, pulled it back and the engine quit. Then he must have panicked (accident report), for he tried to make an emergency landing in rough terrain, but he hit hard and the plane exploded. Another memorial service.

SNJs, formation, acrobatics, touch-and-goes – it did not get any better for a twenty-two-year-old kid (now a man, sic Nuevo Laredo) who had wanted to fly since wet diaper days. It took me ninety-six hours of flying in ten weeks to finish the syllabus. Other than getting laid, sort of, and losing Mass-of-Muscles and some others I did not know well, the most memorable event involved a formation flying session with four Cadets and one exceptional Ensign instructor.

For this venture we were carefully briefed on how to set the SNJ's parking brake, inasmuch as we were going to land at an outlying field where a small refreshment shack awaited student pilots escorted by their instructors. Neat idea.

To preclude having to shut down and restart our planes, which sometimes did not want to start, we would land, taxi up to the small building then all set our parking brakes whilst the SNJs rested at idle power. We would leave the airplanes idling and spend ten or fifteen minutes drinking cokes and peeing. Ensign Nice Guy did it all the time with his students.

Great formation flight and we landed as planned. Funny seeing those five Texans idling away with nobody in the cockpits. But it worked, for a while. As we sat ever so briefly in the building, the barkeep (Coca Cola keep) yelled, "LOOK OUT!" We looked up in horror as one of the SNJs was about to join the party. With a horrendous smashing of glass, the loose aircraft whose brakes were not well set, taxied itself in for a coke. No one hurt except the SNJ, which had a badly chewed up prop, and the building, which needed new front windows.

The enigmatic student flew back with Ensign Nice Guy while the SNJ rested in the bar window. Surprisingly enough, the student was not given a down or punished or anything. He'd had an unblemished record and was three weeks from those precious wings. Ensign Nice Guy took the blame and the practice of parking for cokes with engines idling was stopped. The Cadet with weak brake ankles got his wings with the rest of us. The SNJ party crasher got a new prop and flew home to Kingsville with Ensign Nice Guy driving.

Early in December '44, our group had finished at Kingsville and was transported to Corpus for THE ceremony. Our date of rank was to be 1 December, 1944. In the interim, an exciting event unfolded. Douglas Dauntless SBD-5 dive bombers had arrived at mainside Corpus, and we Cadets were scheduled to fly these machines. SBDs? God, they were the carrier-based dive bombers winning the war in the Pacific and we were going to fly those?

Within a week I had eight flights in SBDs – Cadet Moore yet. As years passed I reflected on that more than once when our squadron in Air Group Five, VF-51, flying F9F-2s off the carrier Essex during the Korean thing in 1951, had a bright young pilot I enjoyed flying with named Armstrong. Midshipman Armstrong, flying combat in jets! Come on! He had his wings but his commission had not come through. Finally, it did and after twenty-some combat missions and one bail-out, Midshipman Armstrong became Ensign Armstrong; Ensign Neil Armstrong, who later scuffed up the moon.

I can tell you to this day where I stood in formation in my seventy-five dollar blues with a gold strip on each sleeve as we Cadets became Ensigns, United States Navy with Wings of Gold proudly displayed on our chests.

The next and most important adventure that would happen in my lifetime occured just three weeks after I was presented my Wings of Gold. I married Marilynn.

We met in 1941 when I was attending the University of Missouri in Rolla (then called the Missouri School of Mines and Metallurgy), and she was a sophomore at Washington University of St. Louis. Before I left for flight training in 1943, I asked her if she would wait for me to win my Navy Wings and commission as Ensign, United States Navy, and then if she would marry me. Marilynn said yes, she would wait, and yes, she would marry me. We were both twenty at that time.

After being commissioned in Corpus Christi I took the train to St. Louis, and in January, 1945, we were married in a lovely church in Webster Groves, Missouri. She was the most beautiful bride, and with great modesty, I must admit that I looked dashing in my Navy blue uniform with one stripe on each sleeve and those elegant gold wings on my chest.

Marilynn could not have been a more wonderful, more beautiful, more fulfilling wife and mother to our four children. Please, dear reader, if nothing else, read chapter 13 of this book. It is about Marilynn, how she lived, how supportive and loving she always was, and how she died in my arms when she was killed . . .

IV

HELLCATS DAY AND NIGHT

Marilynn and I rode the train from St. Louis to Melbourne, Florida, in January of '45 as part of our honeymoon, for me to begin fighter training in the Hellcat at NAS Melbourne in preparation for the Pacific War. The beautiful bride and I moved into a bedroom in Mrs. Nagle's house on Bluff Walk, where we had the run of a bedroom and kitchen privileges, all for sixty dollars a month. Marilynn, who grew up in a lovely home in Webster Groves, Missouri, had earned a Bachelor of Arts degree from Washington University and was accustomed to the nicer things in life, never complained. We didn't have a car for almost a year. Just hitchhiked everywhere we went. My $275 a month Ensign's pay did not go far.

Hellcats at any age were a blast; at my twenty-two years of immaturity they were incredible. The Navy pilots in the Pacific with their F6Fs, together with their F4U Corsairs, could now compete with the Japanese Zeros. It was about time.

With the war still going full blast, it seemed Marilynn and I spent our honeymoon in the Hellcat's cockpit. It was wall-to-wall flying — formation, strafing, air-to-air gunnery, field carrier landing practice, along with sufficient ground school to help us young pilots understand the exigencies of it all.

The final phase of fighter training was car-qual (carrier qualifications), which were conducted on the USS *Solomons*, CVE 67, a jeep carrier about the size of a postage stamp, maybe smaller, out of Ft. Lauderdale. I could not believe how small that carrier looked from 10,000 feet as four of us flew out of NAS Opa Locka for car qual. About 500 feet long, with a landing area almost half that, the *Solomons* was one tiny ship. I made six arrested landings in the Hellcat that day and was deemed carrier qualified. Since then, I have never gotten over my respect for the Navy and Marine pilots who did WW II, and even Korea, off jeep carriers.

The last event of becoming a gen-u-ine fighter pilot was unnerving. From our class of twenty, the Navy needed four volunteers for night-fighter training at NAS Vero Beach. No one volunteered. I was volunteered. I never figured out if it was because I was in the top twenty percent of my class or the bottom twenty percent to be volunteered but I suspected the latter. Wrong stuff strikes again. So it was off to Vero Beach and night fighters.

Marilynn and I packed all our personal belongings in two suitcases and Mrs. Nagle drove us to the bus station for the beginning of our next venture. We bussed to Vero Beach, found a small apartment with our own kitchen, and moved in. Oh, joy.

The unfortunate aspect of night fighters was that they flew at night. On the first day on the job at NAS Vero Beach came the announcement that volunteers were needed to fly the Curtis SB2C Helldivers, which were used as target planes at night in the training program. No one volunteered. I was volunteered yet again. Before my stint in night fighters at Vero was completed, I had logged 250 hours in the Helldiver, all but twenty-five of which were at night.

But it all started in Kingsville, Texas, probably because it was darker there. So before I even cranked up an SB2C or flew an F6F-3N or -5N intercept (Vero had both models), it was off to Kingsville for eight weeks of dark adaptation high above the lush rolling hills of Texas countryside, which we never saw.

One of our group of twenty, a conscientious objector to the night fighter program, was Joe Dean. He had made up his mind after his first night hop in the F6F that it would be his last under the stars. Joe advised our duty flight surgeon his ears ached and his hearing capacity had diminished to dangerously low levels.

The doc could see nothing wrong in Joe's ears but as a precaution of sorts, he painted the insides of Joe's ears with mercurochrome, which made Joe look somewhat like a Choctaw. Joe was advised to stay grounded for a week until his hearing impairment might have time for healing. Joe was so delighted that he went straight to the ship service, bought a bottle of mercurochrome of his own along with some Q-tips, and then awaited a miracle recovery, which he was sure would take weeks, maybe even months.

It took a few days for Joe to learn not to hear, but he soon got pretty good at it. He faithfully painted his ears red twice a day and could only hear when we whispered. The stock question-and-answer scenario around our BOQ went like this:

Question: "Joe, how are your ears ?"

Answer: "Beers? Yes, I'll have one."

Joe never flew again during my eight weeks at Kingsville, and I had no idea of his disposition. It seemed to me that the problem with Joe's approach to avoiding night fighters might well have caused him to swap his Navy Wings of Gold for a broom and a shovel with some cavalry outfit in Texas. Now that is shovelling the wrong stuff.

The first true thrill in our fledgling night hawk group came during the third week at Kingsville. Four of us were checking engines on a taxiway paralleling the duty runway prior to take-off. It was dark. Several hundred yards further down the taxiway was a lone Hellcat whose pilot had been cleared by the tower for take-off. Whereupon the lad spun his machine into position, went to full throttle and started rolling. There was one minor problem. He was still on the taxiway and heading straight for our group of four. I poured the coal to my Hellcat and got the hell off the taxiway onto the grass as did the other three just as the lone eagle roared by, soon to be airborne and thence soon to be grounded. Clearing his "runway" as we did was not without some trauma as the guy next to me taxied into the tail of my machine, throwing metal thereabouts. Nobody hurt except two Hellcats in the grass off the taxiway.

The misguided young aviator was advised by our chief instructor, a be-medalled lieutenant commander, to seek employment elsewhere, perhaps with an amphibious outfit floating offshore Okinawa. I gave the soon-to-be ex-aviator my friend Morris Sievert's location in his LSM anchored near Kadena. Sievert was the exec, engineering officer and sometimes chaplain of his warship, then dodging Kamikazes and preparing for a big invasion of Japan. At Kingsville, our group was down to fifteen pilots from our original twenty. That's not counting out Joe Dean just yet. The number of pilots remaining in the dark would soon be fourteen.

Our eight-week syllabus called for two night cross-country ventures to Oklahoma City and back. We made these round-robins in sections of two planes, landing at Okie City for refueling prior to returning to Kingsville. All we had for navigation was ADF, a low frequency homing device with a needle which would usually, but not always, point to the ground station to which it was tuned. I was wingman on our voyage up to Oklahoma City and leader of our section on the way home during the first of two cross-country exercises.

As we approached NAS Kingsville on our return trip, I could see a solid cloud layer below that had moved in from the bay to tax our navigation skills, such as they were. Approach control advised that the bottom of the cloud layer was 4,000 feet, and with my ADF doing its thing quite well, we descended through the clouds for a safe landing on a very dark night. Before our approach, however, I heard another flight of two call for a steer from the tower since both planes had lost their ADFs. The procedure was simple — the pilot would request a steer, give a long count to ten and back as the ground controller homed in on the pilot's transmission and located the planes. No radar available, but no problems, usually. I heard the tower operator call "180 degree steer," which seemed right to me although I did not know the location of this particular section. It turned out that the 180 degree steer was wrong. The two-plane section had already passed Kingsville and was still headed south. The ground controller had misread his indicator. The steer should have been 360 degrees.

Some fifteen or twenty minutes later, the section leader called for another steer and again was give 180 degrees. They did not know they were down over Mexico. Southern Texas is flat country, but there are hills and mountains not far south of Kingsville in Mexico. Many of the clouds in that part of Mexico have rocks in them, as the saying goes.

Lost and low on fuel, the section leader, thinking he was still over the flat Texas countryside, decided to descend through the clouds and try to figure out where they were. The wingman thought that was a wrong idea and stayed above the clouds on a heading of 180 degrees. Shortly thereafter, the wingman saw a break in the clouds and a city with lights blinking below. He circled through the opening, spotted a small but lighted airfield, and put his F6F down safely on a rather short but adequate asphalt runway. It was midnight and he found himself in a strange part of "Texas" where nobody spoke English.

His section leader had descended through clouds that had rocks in them. The wreckage of his plane was found on a mountainside two days later, and what could be found of his body was bagged and carted down mountain trails on the backs of donkeys. Adios, brave young night-fighter pilot.

We were then at fourteen and counting.

Our group was about to finish the eight-week adventure with thirteen pilots intact. We counted Joe Dean out. Final weeks had included strafing missions on marked targets in the dark of the Texas nights and simulated bombing strikes but no night intercepts. It would soon be back to NAS Vero Beach for that phase of training and into SB2C Helldivers for some of us "volunteers." The biggest problem with night fighters continued to be that they flew at night. Who'd have thought? But we still had one week to go.

An aggressive, extroverted Lieutenant (j.g.) named John Mazza who roomed across from us in the BOQ, was ever ready for the excitement of night fighters and all the goings on in the air after dark. In our last week at Kingsville, we were scheduled for round-robins to several cities nearby, flying our F6Fs separated from one another by staggered take-offs in the dark of night.

John confided in us that he was going to put on a show that night but was secretive about his plan. He said we would find out soon enough. Did we ever. And what a show.

It turned out that he was going to buzz the city of Kingsville at rooftop level (called "flat-hatting" by the Navy) with lights out, full power, max speed. Since there would be about a dozen of us flying around in the region at that time, no one would know, "who done it," as they say. Mazza roared in from the south, flew across the city getting the undivided attention of every citizen below his flight path, and all went well until he encountered Kingsville's water tower. He hit it smack in the middle at an estimated air speed of 300 knots, totally destroying the water tower, the F6F and himself. Some show.

The folks in Kingsville, usually very understanding and hospitable, were not too pleased with this particular nocturnal happening. The Navy personnel immediately responded with water trucks, pumps, pipe-lines, et al., and set out installing a new water tower to make amends as fast as they could for their errant j.g., who was quickly transferred out of night fighters and into Arlington Cemetery. Wrong stuff.

I think most of us, particularly Joe Dean, felt there were enough hazards in night flying without adding the challenges of encounters with water towers, mountains, high tension wires and the like. Those who felt differently were generally weeded out one way or another.

Early on in the night-fighter program at Vero Beach, I was airborne in an SB2C at dusk to serve three hours as target plane for the F6F-3N boys about to depart for the Pacific to win WW II in the night arena. The weather was bright and clear, but my Helldiver's engine was neither. At an altitude of 8,000 feet north of Banana River NAS, the engine gave up what I believed was its last cough. I declared an emergency and headed for NAS Banana River and her 4,000 foot runways.

All went well as my Helldiver rear seat man and I entered the downwind leg for Runway 11 at Banana River, where I dropped wheels and turned into final approach with the fan turning but sounding like it had whooping cough. Touchdown was smooth (of course) as crash trucks and a meatwagon awaited my arrival. Problem. I could not get the machine stopped. Lots of runway lights passed as the end of the runway loomed ahead. There was not enough of it. My machine lumbered into the soft Florida beach sand off the landing strip, lurched to a halt in spectacular fashion with the plane nosing up into an almost vertical pirouette before settling back down to a three-point attitude with no damage occurring to machine or crew.

I climbed heroically out of the cockpit onto the wing to be greeted by the crash crew leader who incredulously inquired if there was a malfunction of my flaps. It seems I had failed to use those landing aids of the SB2C, which was responsible for my running off the runway. It was the flaps' fault! The civilian crash crew patriarch and I chuckled at my stupidity and since there was no damage to anything but my psyche, he avowed he would tell no one and I was declared a hero for having saved the airplane and my ass as well as my crewman's ass.

A few weeks later, I was less heroic. Under the protection of my heavenly friend in the sky, Orion, I was flying practice intercepts in the F6F-3N out over the Gulf Stream when the Hellcat's engine developed herpes. It was about 2 a.m. What to do? Just declare an emergency and head for NAS Banana River. What else? As I approached the field in the darkness, the tower operator who had requested the pilot's name said, "Weren't you just here a few weeks ago?" Deja vu.

For this emergency landing, a mini dead stick, I elected to use all of my Hellcat's landing paraphernalia, including flaps, and did so with success. After a phone call to Marilynn and then a few hours of sleep in the BOQ, I went to the flight line where an instructor pilot from our night-fighter unit sent up from Vero Beach was strapping his omnipotent butt into my Hellcat. He did an engine run-up, checked mags, then called the tower for take-off clearance back to Vero twenty minutes away.

The engine sounded awful to me, but what does an Ensign know? Lieutenant Tommy Thompson — I remember the name — staggered and sputtered into the air in my sick F6F and limped back to Vero. I felt very stupid and very humble.

Tommy and I became friends and crossed paths a number of times in the following two years until he was killed trying to save a sick F4U Corsair. I learned a lot from Tommy in life and in death. Don't be a hero.

In night fighters, a conjugal visit with one's wife was not a scheduled event. Sometimes mid-morning hours were sacred for that lovely union inasmuch as we often spent most of the dark hours prepping for and flying night training missions. Wives understood but found the adaptation process to be difficult and often unfulfilling. Navy pilot wives were mostly loving and beautiful at best, and elegant at worst, and were as understanding as possible in these unnatural circumstances.

On this night, I arrived home at our small apartment in Vero Beach about 3 a.m. after a very dark night in the sky. Since we did not have a car, I walked from the field to my doorstep about two miles away.

Marilynn had been sleeping but awoke with a loving, tender, gentle greeting. After a quick shower it was into bed with this beautiful woman who, to my delight, was wonderfully responsive to my closeness and touch even at some time after 3 a.m. Our union was gentle with a completeness that can take two lovers into a trance of oneness where they feel as if the two had indeed become one. So it was in these early morning hours with us. After an eternity of soft passion I suddenly became fulfilled with a burst of energy and pleasure followed by complete relaxation. Within moments, I fell sound asleep still on top of and coupled with my loving young wife. Shortly thereafter I was awakened by her sobbing as she was trying to cry without waking me.

I thought I had hurt her. I had. She could not understand how I could fulfill myself with little apparent caring for her own needs. She was disappointed, unfulfilled and hurt. How could I?

Thereafter, no matter how tired, how drained or how emotionally traumatized I might become in the flying world, I never did that again.

There was a quiet, simplistic, almost ethereal aspect to flying night intercepts. There was only the ground controller, the airplane and the pilot. Those factors almost transcended the ominous darkness in which night-fighter pilots practiced their trade. But it was an awesome environment for this twenty-two-year-old Ensign learning the business of flying Hellcats off a carrier at midnight, locating and destroying an enemy plane, then returning to the carrier in the early morning hours.

The SB2Cs served well as target planes for our practice intercepts, for they were equipped with flame dampers on their exhaust stacks, flew lights off, and emitted not one candelabra of light. For a "tallyho," the intercept pilot had to obtain a visual on the Helldiver, which often meant closing to within less than 100 feet from the target plane and having to be directly under it to see its silhouette against the stars.

A typical intercept started with the ground controller giving directional vectors to the pilot until he could pick up the target on his cockpit radar scope, usually in the six-to-eight-mile range. The pilot would report the contact then continue the intercept using his own radar and instruments until he got a "tallyho."

It was a bit hairy for the target plane crew as it watched the Hellcat with its running lights approach the SB2C, sometimes getting dangerously close. The rear seat man in the target plane was armed with a spotlight, which he could shine onto the interceptor if it came too close for comfort, telling the Hellcat pilot to get his ass outta there.

Unfortunately a few unseemly contacts occurred during my tour at Vero with F6F-3Ns or -5Ns chewing tails off SB2Cs which caused much foul language and a few casualties. A good friend, Bill Preston, flying targets one night over central Florida had the tail of his SB2C chewed off by a Hellcat. Bill bailed out successfully and spent the night feeding marsh mosquitoes in the Everglades about a mile from the F6F pilot who was doing the same thing

— no helos in those days. There was no answer as to why the rear seat man did not use his spotlight; his 'chute didn't open.

The delicacy of the intercept generated an unusual camraderie between pilot and ground controller. I felt as if I knew all our group of controllers very well and as close friends although I never met one of them in person. The intercept process for me was a ballet at night witnessed only by my friend, the constellation Orion, and the other stars and the moon. For the SB2C driver there was not much fun in being hunted because the process was fraught with uncertainties and danger.

The final chapter of becoming a qualified night-fighter pilot as it were, was making night carrier landings on the same postage stamp wallowing in the Gulf Stream, the USS *Solomon*. For me, it was hard to find it in daylight. At night, it took all the help I could get from Genesis, Exodus, Leviticus and Deuteronomy to find the Numbers on the carrier, much less land on it. Unforgettable.

I left the night-fighter training program at the age of twenty-two going on thirty-five to join VF(N)-90 at NAS Boca Chica near Key West, Florida. VF(N)-90 was a staging squadron from which contingents of eight or ten night-fighter pilots would be formed for assignment to the carriers at war in the Pacific.

Shortly after Marilynn and I arrived in Key West, Hiroshima and Nagasaki were hit by atomic bombs and the Japanese surrendered. Several months later, I was ordered to VBF-20, a squadron of Grumman F8F-1 Bearcats assigned to Air Group Nine and the carrier *Philippine Sea*, CVA-47. The Air Group was based in Charleston, Rhode Island, and so it was northward to commence a love affair with a Bearcat.

V

BEARCATS

Today in 1995, the F8F Bearcat holds the world's speed record for propeller-driven airplanes. I had the privilege of driving the F8F-1 out of NAS Charleston, Rhode Island, for two years – a year of which I spent with my squadronmates flying off the USS *Philippine Sea*, CV-47, in the Mediterranean and elsewhere. A little tough on our families at home, but exciting flying. In this period between 1946 and '48, I logged more than one hundred carrier landings in the Bearcat on the *Phil Sea*, a straight deck carrier with a lot of class, which qualifies me as a Centurion in the Tailhook Association, an organization of which I am a proud member.

The Bearcat, for all its great qualities as a fighter plane, killed too many pilots. It was very small with a lot of power and a huge four-bladed prop. In the carrier approach, if a pilot got slow and poured the coal to it, the plane easily torque-rolled, which put the machine and pilot upside down in the ocean, almost always fatal. We lost two pilots from our squadron that way, and one of our other squadrons lost its Skipper in the same fashion. He lived above our apartment in Wickford, Rhode Island, so we felt the pain acutely. Devastating to his wife and new baby. Tough on Marilynn as well. Too close to home.

We had three World War II combat veterans in our squadron, one of whom I flew with frequently as his wingman, Lieutenant (j.g.) Harry J. Sundberg. One afternoon, he and I were landing at Charlie Town, he first. Shortly after touchdown, I watched from a few hundred yards behind as his plane veered rather sharply to the left, ran off the runway and turned upside down after the Bearcat's wheels dug into the sand. Brake failure. As I passed by his F8F, I saw in horror fuel pouring out of its belly tank, covering the cockpit area and vaporizing over the hot exhaust stacks. I turned off the runway, and taxied back to a point about 200 yards from Sundberg's plane, and stopped. From out of nowhere came a pickup truck, well before the crash trucks arrived, and the driver leaped out of his truck, grabbed a shovel and started digging.

Incredibly, he was digging a trench to the cockpit in the same soft sand which had caused the plane to overturn. In moments, with sand flying everywhere, he had dug a trench to the smashed cockpit covered with high octane fuel as Sundberg hung upside down by his seat belt and shoulder straps. As I reflect now on the episode, it seems like slow motion. When the trench was completed to the cockpit, Sundberg unbuckled his seat belt and lowered his body onto his shoulders. The shoveler grabbed him and pulled him from under the Bearcat through the trench.

As the crash trucks and meatwagon came racing down the runway, Sundberg and the shoveler were on their feet running from the airplane. Seconds later, there was a "whoosh" – not a "bang" – and the Bearcat was engulfed in the dark red and black flames of a fire fueled by high octane gasoline. The Bearcat and the truck were consumed in the holocaust even as the crash trucks arrived.

In the ready room, Sundberg treated the event as it if were just another flight. Scared me and I was fearless then. We made the shoveler an honorary member of our squadron.

Early in our flight training program, we had a week of night flying in the F8Fs. Each pilot was scheduled for three familiarization flights just to meet the darkness with these wonderful fighters. There were no landing lights on these planes, just as there were none on any carrier based flying machines. I was fairly acclimated to the night environment thanks to more than a year in night fighters, but many of our new pilots were not. So it was an adventure.

After two flights, I was assigned as duty officer in the control tower during night ops because I had more night hours than almost everyone else in the squadron, maybe also because I was an ensign and our exec thought I'd be out of the way up in the tower. My second night of duty up there was not a good one. It was very dark – clear but black. The great little Bearcat had two features which could be troublesome. First, as mentioned earlier, it was easy to torque-roll the plane in the approach configuration. Second, in this configuration, the Bearcat had neutral longitudinal stability from about 100 knots to stall, which was 65 to 68 knots. To the pilots this meant one could not judge airspeed by the feel of the control stick. It felt the same at 70 knots as it did at 100 knots. We all learned quickly to monitor the airspeed indicator throughout the landing approach. On this night, one of our pilots apparently did not.

About nine o'clock, Lieutenant Al Elpern, with new Wings of Gold, called the tower reporting that he was at angels 5 returning to the base because of a rough running engine. I ordered a deferred emergency, alerting the crash crews as Elpern passed overhead before breaking port to the downwind leg at 1,000-feet altitude. It was so dark we could not see the fighter – only its running lights, red and green on wingtips and white on the tail.

On the downwind leg, he seemed slow to the three of us in the tower but I was not sure enough of this to call him and tell him to check his airspeed. Goddamn it. Moments later, the Bearcat suddenly stopped in mid-air and all we saw were red and green wingtip running lights spiraling straight downward from 1,000 feet. He was spinning. In only seconds, there was a terrific explosion and fireball as the plane impacted the ground. The fire, fueled by high-octane gas, was an inferno. There would be no possibility of survival unless Al had managed to bail out, which was extremely unlikely. There was not enough time or altitude for that miracle. (No ejection seats in those days.)

I left the tower and climbed into a crash truck enroute to the scene. I wanted to be sure there was a search of the area in the event Al had made it out in a 'chute, but the search was fruitless. When the fire was finally extinguished, there was nothing but rubble illuminated by the spotlights from firetrucks. In what had been a cockpit could be seen a body burned beyond recognition.

The next day, as squadron maintenance officer, I was at the crash site responsible for having the rubble loaded onto a flatbed truck for disposition at the Quonset Point scrapheap. In the process, I discovered one of Al's shoes which apparently had been blown clear of the wreckage. Picking it up, my first thought was to return it to his widow but I quickly realized that would serve no purpose, would be hurtful and even cruel. So I threw it onto the flatbed with the rest of the rubble. Then I cried.

75

We had been training and flying hard in the Bearcat in preparation for carrier qualifications (car-quals) and subsequent deployment on *Philippine Sea*, CVA-47, destined for the Mediterranean via Guantanamo, Cuba. While practicing tactics with four plane divisions, we ran into a very bad day.

Our Skipper, Commander Jennings, took off with his division as did our Exec, Lieutenant Commander Little, for some dogfighting practice, Jennings' division being the aggressors and the Exec's gang the defenders. I was airborne on a post-maintenance check flight but was monitoring the action on our squadron frequency. The usual banter could be heard: "bogies incoming at one o'clock," "turn into them – turn into them." Then a transmission, more a scream than a call: "Mayday, Mayday – Mid-air, Mid-air." Then some more transmissions I do not recall, but it was frightening.

Our Skipper and our Executive Officer had collided almost head-on. There was nothing but junk in the air as airplane pieces floated and fell 10,000 feet into the sea off Block Island. Nothing was recovered. No airplane parts, no bodies, nothing. It was more than incredulous. It was unbelievable.

In the weeks which followed, we had an obligation to regroup and carry on, but it wasn't easy. Out of the gloom and aftermath of this tragic accident came a blessing for our squadron. Our new Skipper came on board, Stanley "Swede" Vjetesa. What a man he was and what a pilot. Swede had become a double ace in the Pacific, and coming aboard, with his leadership and fighter pilot skills, was a panacea for all. And so we put the tragedy behind us, as best we could, and prepped for our ventures to Getmo and the Med.

In our training prior to embarking on *Phil Sea*, we had our guns loaded up and we proceeded in flights of four (a division) to a gunnery range in the hills of New Hampshire. On this day, we had two divisions enroute to what would be our first live strafing runs at the well-marked ground targets in this lovely rolling terrain.

I followed with another ensign, a guy named Sanderson, on our second run and was no more than a thousand feet behind and to his port side. I stopped firing and was ready to pull out of the dive while Sandy was still blasting away at the target. It was obvious he was going to fly straight into the mini-mountain. I started to yell at him to pull out, when suddenly there were vapor trails from each wingtip as he started pulling up, then no wingtips at all! The outer wing panels had peeled off and it looked to me as if he were flying a wingless plane. Sandy cleared the hill, barely.

Good old Grumman Ironworks, makers of the Bearcat and other great fighting machines, had been clever with this one. To make the plane as light as possible, yet rugged, they had designed the wings so that if a pilot exceeded nine G, the outer three feet (approximate – I don't remember exactly) of each wing would just break away instead of the entire wing failing. We were aware of this design characteristic but who would pull nine G? I'd never been to nine G in my career except in a centrifuge. Sandy had – his accelerometer showed 9.5 G, so no wing outer panels. I saw one of the tips sail by as I pulled out, but the awesome sight was that Bearcat with such stubby wings. Sandy knew what had happened and radioed he was okay and that the plane was flying okay.

I escorted him back to our base in Charlie Town where he dropped wheels and flaps and checked stall speeds. His landing was a success with his touchdown about 20 knots faster than norm.

Another pilot in a different F8F squadron was involved in a similar circumstance except that when he exceeded nine G in his dive, only the right wing panel broke away, which rolled him to the right straight into the ground. It took Grumman about a week to resolve that dilemma. They designed and modified the Bearcats with pertinent explosives, switches and wiring so that if one panel failed and detached under stress, the other panel was blown off by charges. Good old Corky Meyer, Grumman's chief test pilot extraordinaire, tested the rigging, which worked just fine. I know for certain that Sandy never pulled nine G again.

Carrier qualifications in the F8F aboard the *Phil Sea* were a blast. We had to successfully make eight arrested landings in daylight hours and two in darkness to be declared qualified. For me, after having made night landings on the 500 foot *Solomons*, it seemed that landing on the *Phil Sea* would be like landing on I-10 somewhere between Jacksonville and Tallahassee. Yet, however qualified one might be in night landings on a straight-deck carrier, there was always a potential for seepage of urine somewhere in the landing pattern at night.

During my quals, I ran afoul of Swede, who was never one to get angry, but rather firm in doing things Swede's way. After my fourth arrested landing, my deck take-off greeted me with some engine missing noises and fussings that were attention getters. With extraordinary heroism, I said nothing and continued sporting around the pattern for another arrested landing, which was successful. However, from the moment I pulled the throttle to idle at the cut until the Bearcat was stopped by the arresting gear, flames poured out of the left engine exhaust stacks and were blown into the cockpit by the slightly left crosswind always provided by the carrier to keep us clear of stack-wash.

Fortunately, I knew exactly how to handle this situation. I went to full throttle to get the engine running again, which would eliminate the flames and allow me to be back in control. Unfortunately, the engine didn't give a damn about the throttle position as the prop windmilled and continued to throw flames into the cockpit. It seemed prudent to me that I should abandon ship; whereupon I unbuckled, leaped out onto the starboard wing and thence to the flight deck.

Within moments as I was ambling away from the fiery machine still wearing my 'chute, I heard a momentary engine roar as if the engine was trying to come to life. Then I realized I had left the Bearcat with the prop turning and the throttle full open and no one in the cockpit. With a mighty leap I was back up on the wing to the cockpit where I reached through the flames to grab the mixture control and pull it to "off." The flames hadn't stopped, but the Bearcat had started to taxi forward all by its lonesome. Fortunately, pulling the mixture to "off" stopped the engine and the Bearcat before it destroyed the island structure of the carrier.

In sick bay, the flight surgeon gently applied unguentine or equivalent to my slightly seared face and gave me a mini two-ounce bottle of brandy. The right thing to do. Medicine at its best. It would not be the last time I would be burned nor the last time medicinal brandy would be applied for the psyche.

Swede was less than tolerant. He advised me in his gentle, fatherly way that if I ever did that again I might seek employment with the Coast Guard or the Air Force because I would no longer be needed in Naval aviation. The greasy unguentine on my face was of no help. Wrong stuff.

On our first Air Group venture aboard the *Phil Sea* before departing for the Mediterranean via Getmo, we had a group grope at sea off Bermuda.

All was well as we launched everything but the captain's gig – smooth seas, light winds, sunny skies – great day for the grope.

For reasons known only to meteorologists and other mystics, we had only been airborne about an hour before the seas changed markedly and inexplicably to an ocean surface that looked like a washboard from the air and more like a coronary to the carrier's skipper and air boss. There were no whitecaps, but a rolling ocean surface with evenly spaced swells some fifteen feet in height and off the surface wind about forty-five degrees. It looked ominous from the air and from the Captain's bridge as well. (Later, it was attributed to an earthquake deep in the Bermuda Triangle.)

The decision was made to recover aircraft ASAP, starting with the Bearcats, all forty of them, many of which did not have belly tanks and thus were fuel critical. I was in a Bearcat with an external tank and was thus relegated to the last group of twelve with belly tanks to be recovered. From my perch at 12,000 feet overhead, I watched the first F8F come aboard and disintegrate from its impact with the carrier deck, which was rolling and pitching unpredictably with a morbid magnitude. The pilot was not injured but the Bearcat was on her belly, crumpled and mortally wounded. Problem was, it took agonizing minutes for the ship's deck crane (Tilly) to remove the Bearcat from the landing area to permit recovering the fuel-starved F8Fs and their very anxious pilots.

The air boss's admonition to conserve fuel was received in our ear phones as only confirmation of what we already knew. The twelve of us with belly tanks were more comfortable than the twenty-seven without, but not much.

Three more fighters made it safely aboard this straight-deck carrier before another slammed into the rolling deck, had its landing gear smashed, and ended up upside down in the barrier. Those airborne, conserve fuel.

The SB2C bombers and the TBM torpeckers had ample fuel reserves that allowed them to orbit *Philippine Sea* with some degree of comfort. Although we were out of range for landings in Bermuda and had no sister carrier alongside, those guys had fuel to burn, as they say, but we fighter pilots had a major problem.

An hour and a half after we had commenced recovering the fighters, it was my turn. There were two of us still airborne in Bearcats and I was not flush with fuel. My belly tank had been long empty and I had twenty-five gallons of petrol remaining according to my fuel gauge, which had better not be lying.

On my first pass, it became abundantly clear why so many F8Fs had succumbed to the carrier's rolling, pitching deck. I was waved off in the groove as the deck rolled perhaps fifteen degrees and dropped precipitously away from me. Two passes later, I took a cut from the LSO and picked up the number one wire as the deck rose to greet my Bearcat. Just as well because I did not have enough fuel for another pass. My machine was intact but our two squadrons sent eleven F8Fs to overhaul following their encounters with the angry ocean. The SB2C Helldivers and TBM Avengers fared a little better, sending only five to overhaul as escorts to our Bearcats. Only one pilot was killed – although I hate the word "only." One is too many.

When the carrier dropped anchor in the harbor at Guantanamo Bay, Cuba, and the liberty bell clanged, "all ashore that's going ashore," was the signal for those free of shipboard duties and entitled to a night on the town, as it were. The town was Caminera, just outside the Naval base, and it was known as "Caminooch."

Many of the crew decided to visit this garden spot after a few beers at the Officers and Enlisted Mens clubs, mostly out of curiosity and mayhaps for a bit of shopping. Our exec advised me that I would be the officer-in-charge of the shore patrol detail in Caminooch for our first night ashore, leading me to conclude that I must have done something wrong.

So off we shore patrollers went via liberty boats to Getmo and thence to Caminooch. I was dressed in my dashing white uniform with Ensign bar and gold wings bedecked; a black arm band on my left arm identifying me as commandant of the shore patrol unit. I also had this distinguished assignment our second night in port because, as our Exec said, I was then the most experienced. So much for experience.

The town of Caminooch turned out to be nothing but a huge brothel with dirt streets and probably fifty bars, all of which were surrounded by small rooms, about eight by twelve feet in size, equipped with a bed and a broad. Also in this homey village were two prophylactic stations (pro stations) manned by Navy corpsmen available for those who might be tempted to commit an indiscretion of some kind and perhaps encounter the wrong stuff. The maidens came in all sizes, shapes and ages and, not surprisingly, were quite friendly.

During my two-night tour of duty, I was privileged to observe some lovelies who were exceptionally successful at what they did; several having guys unabashedly lined up awaiting a turn for their services. One girl, named Maria, was very pretty, bleached blond, nice body, nice smile, very attractive and very busy. I watched her accommodate three sailors and one j.g. in an hour. I knew what she was doing but couldn't figure out how she could do it so fast. I think she planned to buy a bank in Havana when she turned twenty.

I found Caminooch to be a broadening experience, but I did not plan to go back. As they say – twice is enough.

On a sunny afternoon out of Getmo, four of us took off from the *Phil Sea* scheduled for a two-and-one-half-hour Combat Air Patrol (CAP) mission over our small task force. This, of course, required belly tanks since the flight was rather long for both Bearcat and pilot. Our leader was Lieutenant Bob Hunt and I was flying section leader as Bob guided us three ensigns through the simulated combat mission.

We were chugging along at 10,000 feet in a rather loose formation scanning the skies for potential enemy airplanes, the closest of which was more than five thousand miles away. It was then I was privileged to witness one of the most extraordinary aerial feats in the annals of Naval aviation.

The Bearcat cockpit was quite small, like that of the Douglas A-4 which was to come along later. Our leader, Lieutenant Hunt, waved us a bit farther out from his plane and then made one terse radio transmission: "I'll be busy for a few minutes." Nothing further.

I watched as his flying became somewhat erratic and noticed he was trying to take off his flight suit. First one arm, then the next, then a bare upper body. In a Bearcat? Whatever was going on? His flight continued to be erratic but safe, it seemed, yet I was not comfortable about the scene and called him on the radio. His reply was simply an order to stay off the air.

After a few minutes of this strange airshow, he opened the canopy of the plane and threw something out of the cockpit, which cleared the tail and went on its way to the ocean below. That was followed by his struggling back into his flight suit and then business as usual.

It was only after we returned aboard ship and were debriefing in our ready room that we learned what had transpired. Bob had to make feces. We all know that bowels sometimes move in mysterious ways and this was his day for mystery. In that tiny cockpit he had declothed, defecated carefully into his undershirt, disposed of the waste over the side, reclothed, and flown on.

81

None of us had guessed this as we observed this extraordinary feat but he had done it. The debriefing was brief – Bob wanted to get into the shower.

Our air group was destroying targets on the island of Vieques off Puerto Rico in preparation for the upcoming Mediterannean cruise in late 1947, when the *Philippine Sea* made a scheduled, albeit brief, stop at Roosevelt Roads, a Navy facility on the east coast of Puerto Rico. As the planes in the air were being recovered on the carrier prior to making port, one of our pilots reported a rough running engine in his Bearcat and was vectored to the airport at the Roads. Accompanying the young Ensign was Lieutenant (j.g.) "Goose" Gossage in another F8F, and they made it safely to the landing strip as *Phil Sea* docked nearby.

Phil Sea would only be berthed for forty-eight hours, so we sent a maintenance troubleshooting group up to the airfield to restore health to the ailing Bearcat's R-2800 engine in order that the two airplanes could be recovered aboard the carrier when she got underway. A test flight was scheduled after the repair work was ostensibly accomplished and the two Bearcats taxied out for a flight check.

During run-up, the ailing Bearcat was reported still ailing, but Goose, in his plane was ready and charged up, and decided to go ahead and get airborne for a short boondoggle around the Puerto Rico airspace. He also decided to put on a mini airshow for those who had not seen this elegant airplane perform. And did he ever. He got airborne, sucked up his wheels, gained some speed, pulled her up and did a slow roll on take-off. It probably was the most awesome flight performance any of the onlookers had ever seen because he didn't make it. At the bottom of his roll, he impacted the ground and the plane exploded as they almost always do. Goose was killed instantly. Some show.

The next day *Philippine Sea* was going to get underway as scheduled. Swede called me to the ready room and advised me that I would be driven to the airport about two miles up a dirt road, and that I was to get the other Bearcat back to the ship and he didn't care how – either fly it back, truck it back or whatever. After all, I was the maintenance officer. Just get it back to the ship, he said, because we needed it for the six months we would spend defending the U.S.A.'s interests in the Mediterranean. That was an, "Aye, aye, Skipper."

My plan was to make a check flight then fly the plane aboard the carrier the following morning as she got underway. The best laid plans of moose and men oft go awry, as they say.

I cranked up the Bearcat and the engine made sounds I had never heard before. I wouldn't have even cut the grass with it. There was no way I would fly that invalid aboard the carrier the next day. After all, I didn't make it all the way up to Ensign by being stupid.

The local *policia* were understanding. One of them took me in his patrol car onto the route down the winding dirt road from the airport to the carrier's dockage, about two miles as the snake crawls. What I wanted to see was whether I could taxi the ill Bearcat, with wings folded, down the road to home since there were no tractors or tow bars available. It seemed plausible, so that became "le plan."

It was a bumpy, dusty ride around some sharp corners on the rutted dirt road, but the Bearcat seemed much happier taxiing than flying, as was I.

Aboard ship all the crew could see was a massive dust storm winding through the hills toward *Phil Sea*, having no idea of its origin. Soon hundreds of crew members manned the flight deck to observe the phenomenon, only to watch an oncoming patrol car, lights flashing, being followed by a dusty Bearcat, which was taxiing around the last corner to the pier.

As I parked the machine at the number two elevator and shut her down, I looked up to see Swede standing on the elevator, arms folded, with a big smile on his face. That said it all. No waving, no hand-clasping over head, no high fives – just a big smile. More than enough.

That evening the sick Bearcat was hoisted aboard, and we set sail the next day for the Mediterranean, minus one plane and one fine pilot left in the memories of Roosevelt Roads.

We had bombed and strafed Vieques, a target island east of Puerto Rico, but not without incident. One of our lads had run amok with his machine guns and strafed an observation tower on the outskirts of the bombing range with considerable success. Fortunately, the crew which normally manned the tower was not on station, but radios and other electronic gear therein did not fare well. Swede was pissed. Other than that we were fairly intact and well-trained for the rigors of six months in the Mediterranean. We would miss "Goose."

First stop, Gibraltar. Big rock. From there other aircraft carriers had visited some lovely cities: Marseille, Athens, Cairo, Cannes. The *Philippine Sea* must have drawn the short straw, for we visited such glamorous places as Bone, Algeria; Sfax, Tunisia; the island fortresses of Heraculon and Argestole, Cephalonia; and anchored off the coast of Tripoli, which was adorned with many sunken ships that had fared poorly in World War II. All in all, it was not a scenic tour.

At many ports of call, the ship had to anchor more than 15 miles off shore because of shallow water. That made for some rough liberty boat ventures with lots of seasickness which took much of the fun out of going ashore.

Naples was a welcomed change. We tied up dockside there for instant access to taxis, pubs, and pretty Italian girls, many of whom fell madly in love with the American boys and their bags of lira. My quest was different. I wanted to buy an accordion. No problema. A cabby took me straight to a music store where I became enamored with a full-size, 120 base, Scandali accordion, color red.

I couldn't play it, but no matter. It would be mine if I could afford it. Some dickering settled the price at twenty cartons of American cigarettes that would have to be smuggled off the ship, which was slightly against Navy regs. But moneywise I could afford it with Lucky Strike cigarettes selling for fifty-five cents a carton aboard ship. It only took me four trips from the ship to the music store with five cartons of Luckies taped to my chest and legs each trip under my Navy greens. So for eleven dollars and some loose lira for taxi fare, the beautiful Scandali was mine. Its tone is as beautiful today as it was when I bought it almost fifty years ago. I still can't play it.

From the flying standpoint it was not all fun and games in the air. Although World War II had been over for more than two years, there remained enough turmoil in countries on the shores of the Med to keep our air group on alert and flying with machine guns loaded and ready. And of course, at the end of a flight, there was always the need to land aboard, safely, if possible.

One afternoon we launched a group grope off Malta – every plane that would fly airborne – and for this all of us in Bearcats carried a belly tank to provide enough petrol for the three-hour mission. The belly tank had no fuel gauge indication for the pilot in the cockpit so its use was very simple: you just selected "belly tank" and flew on it until the engine quit, then shifted over to the main tank. Needless to say, it was better that this transition occur at altitude rather than in the landing pattern.

On this grope, I was one of the first to come aboard and after dropping off my flight gear in the ready room, grabbed my trusty unautomatic 35 mm Ansco 3C camera and went topside to vulture's row to take Kodachromes of my returning squadronmates. By happenstance, I was focused on Lieutenant Kirk Hershey in his F8F on the crossleg of his approach when his plane suddenly fell out of the sky, generated a horrendous splash, flipped upside down and sank in less than twenty seconds. The only thing that came to the surface was Kirk, all 230 pounds of him, which had to be put into the Bearcat cockpit with a shoehorn. How he squeezed out of the thing underwater I don't know, but I got it on film.

Our destroyer escort, or plane guard (no helos then), spotted his bobbing head and shortly afterward pulled Kirk safely aboard, abused only by a two inch gash on his forehead. Kirk had been an All-American football star at Cornell, had played pro ball with the Philadelphia Eagles, was as gentle as he was big and tough, and fortunately had a sense of humor as big as his heart. Getting him back aboard the carrier, however, turned out to be a problem – not mechanical or physical, but one of diplomacy.

It was customary for a carrier at sea to send a sizeable can of ice cream over to a destroyer by high line in exchange for the transfer of a rescued pilot back to the carrier by boatswains chair. But in this instance, the destroyer skipper, in sizing up Kirk, radioed that he demanded an equal amount of ice cream, i.e., 230 pounds, chocolate or strawberry, for Kirk's return. Our captain, knowing that Kirk was okay and that our crew of 3,500 men would enjoy the radio communications between the two ship captains, switched the ship's radio to the public address system so all aboard could enjoy the conversation. There was some delightful banter between our ship's captain and the destroyer's C.O. related to the rescued pilot, which culminated in our summarily advising the destroyer they could keep Kirk. He wasn't worth 230 pounds of ice cream.

The problem was resolved. We transferred a negotiated amount of chocky ice cream to the "tin can" and got back a still wet Kirk Hershey with a stitched gash on his forehead and a huge smile on his face.

The celebration in our ready room was typical fun and intimidations. We accused Kirk of forgetting to shift his fuel selector from belly tank to main and running his tank dry in the landing pattern, which he vehemently denied. His answer told it all: "If you don't believe me, go raise the plane and check it for yourselves." The Bearcat rested on the bottom of the Mediterranean in 5,000 feet of water.

Upon our air group's return from its six-month cruise, I flew off the carrier in a Bearcat to our home base in Charlie Town, and as I taxied in to park my plane I was astounded to find my taxi director was – Marilynn, eight months pregnant, giving me the correct signals: when to turn, where to stop, when to cut engine! Beautiful. All well-staged, each pilot who flew in had his wife, mom or girlfriend park his plane. It could not have been more elegant. Good old Navy!

Shortly afterward, four of our pilots were invited to go to NAS Quonset Point to check out in the new jet fighters, which were first to enter the fleet: the FH-1 Phantom made by McDonnell, a twin jet machine that turned out to be the smoothest airplane I had ever flown. As Marilynn whiled away her final hours before giving birth to our first son in 1948, I was privileged to fly my first jet – a thrill hard to describe even today. What a welcome home that was!

VI

HELLO JETS

From FH-1 Phantoms to a year in the Navy's General Line School in Newport, Rhode Island. Man, oh, manachevitz, what a dichotomy for the average aviator. In between learning about damage control on a destroyer and how to load 16 inch cannons on a battle wagon, I got to fly SNJs, twin Beachcrafts and an occasional Hellcat all of four hours a month aggregate. Flight pay requirements. I flew just enough to be dangerous.

After graduating from General Line School (everyone graduated), I received orders to the training command in Pensacola. I must have flunked something.

Marilynn and I moved to Pensacola with young son, Randy, and bought a frame house in Navy Point outside the main gate at Pensy for a downpayment of $275 and payments of $60 monthly, which fit my $500-a-month lieutenant junior grade income very well. The foundation of the house was laid on a sizeable family of termites, which supported it nicely while we lived there.

Upon completion of instructor schooling at Mainside Pensy, it was on to NAS Whiting Field where I was condemned for two years to the rear seat of SNJs from which visibility was eternally zero. No matter – up front was some kid who had never flown an airplane. He would show the way.

We sold the house in Navy Point, for $275 no less, and moved to Milton, Florida, close to Whiting Field. I was never too good at real estate. So we moved into our new cottage in Milton and I was off to a full day's work in the ass end of SNJs at Whiting.

I was just coming out of shock after two weeks of this foolishness when, following a typical instructional flight, I was gently explaining to the cadet of the moment what a total idiot he was, that his mother may have had canine genes, and that in a word, he was hopeless. All this intellectual diatribe was interrupted by a messenger with a summons ordering me to the commanding officer's omnipotent presence with haste. With great haste, in fact.

Although I could think of a dozen things I had done wrong over the past few days, I could not recall any which would invoke such an invitation to the Skipper's office.

Entering the marble halls into the presence of "Numero Uno," I was invited to stand at ease.

"Moore," sez the Skipper, a burly commander, "our records indicate you have flown jets. Is that true?"

"Yes, sir – the FH-1 Phantom."

"Moore," Skipper said, "you are the only pilot we can find in the training command here who has flown jets. Would you like to be a jet instructor?"

"Yes, Sir, Sir," sez I.

It seemed that the Navy's first Jet Training Unit, JTU-1, was coming to Whiting Field and needed five instructor pilots to supplement their cadre of ten already on board where they were located, then somewhere in Texas. I was to be one of the five. Thank you, FH-1 Phantom. Thank you. Thank you. Thank you.

The TO-1, Navy's designation of the Air Force F-80, was a single-seat jet we would use to teach young and old Naval aviators alike how to fly jets. I had been removed from the SNJ's rear seat tomb. It turned out that this single event changed the course of my life forever.

Getting out of the rear cockpit of the SNJ into the TO-1 Shooting Star (Air Force F-80) in the fall of 1949 was analogous to climbing out of a Model T Ford into a '95 Cadillac with the North Star System – whatever that is. JTU-1 arrived at Whiting Field in style with Lieutenant Commander V.P. "Red" O'Neil in charge, and I was privileged to join his team as a bone-i-fide jet instructor. At least in the TO-1 I could see where I was going in the air.

The training syllabus encompassed thirty days of ground school and flying with each student logging about thirty hours in the silver bird during that time. It was markedly different then, than in these days. The TO-1 Shooting Star was an Air Force single-seated fighter. A student's first jet flight, be he a shiny new Ensign or a four-striper, was solo. It was three days of ground school and cockpit checkouts and then it was into the blue with you. No duel instruction in flight, no touch-and-gos with an instructor yelling obscenities from a rear cockpit. The Shooting Star was a little short of rear cockpits. That didn't happen until the great T-33 trainers made the scene. I had 250 hours in the F-80 before I flew the T-33.

The scheme worked amazingly well. We processed a new class of some twenty students every thirty days and I do not recall losing a student during the two and a half years I was there, although we did lose an instructor, Johnny Lanning.

Regarding Johnny's death, the TO-1s we flew had suspect cockpit pressurization systems, in large part because of canopy seals that didn't seal much. A pilot might be at 35,000 feet and have the cockpit pressurized to 28,000 feet instead of 16,000 feet as it should be. Without supplemental oxygen through the pilot's oxygen mask, that could be fatal very quickly.

Lanning was returning to Whiting Field from Nashville, cruising along at 33,000 feet, when he apparently lost consciousness from hypoxia. Observers on the ground reported an F-80 dived almost straight into the ground near Montgomery, Alabama. From the wreckage of Johnny's TO-1 (F-80) it could not be determine if his oxygen mask had been properly connected to its supply hoses in the cockpit. Medical examinations of what tissues of his body could be recovered indicated oxygen starvation – hypoxia. So somewhere enroute, the oxygen supply system, coupled with questionable cockpit pressurization levels, took the life of a fine pilot.

Out of this accident and similar ones came an innovative design incorporated into the military airplane's oxygen supply equipment. The pilot's oxygen mask hose connectors were redesigned with a fitting such that if the hose were not properly connected to the cockpit oxygen supply, the pilot could not inhale. That simple gadget saved a lot of lives.

Later in my flying career, I had an interesting encounter with hypoxia, which to me was not only informative but probably life-saving as well. At the Naval Air Test Center at Patuxent River, while I was at the Test Pilot School, I was practicing speed powers in the F-86 Sabre at 25,000 feet – a simple test designed to measure airplane performance under given conditions such as known altitude, temperatures, power settings and weight/center-of-gravity parameters. My cockpit pressurization was minimal with the cockpit altimeter reading 20,500 feet, but my breathing was normal and I was not aware of any oxygen problems. Yet I seemed incapable of flying the F-86 any closer to 25,000 than plus or minus thirty feet, inadequate for acceptable performance data. Then I noticed that my vision was narrowing in scope – tunnel vision. At that time it occurred to me I might not be getting adequate oxygen, so I checked the oxygen supply blinker indicator which is designed to close, or blink, on each inhalation IF the pilot is getting oxygen. It was not moving as I inhaled. But the message I got from that was almost fatal. My oxygen starved brain concluded that the blinker was broken and that I had to remember to report that malfunction upon landing. Then I resumed the test, trying to stabilize my altitude exactly on 25,000 feet. Just before passing out as best I could tell, some intuitive impulse told me I was in real trouble and so I rolled into a split ess, dove vertically through 12,000 feet before leveling out at 6,000 feet where my vision and powers of intelligence returned with the influx of oxygen to my system. On the ground, it was determined that the F-86 oxygen system had indeed failed. It was a lesson well-learned related to the onset of hypoxia and its often fatal ramifications.

On a happier note at JTU-1, we had an incident in the TO-1 piloted by a student named Lieutenant Bob McBride. He came to us for a checkout in jets with a fighter pilot background and almost 1,500 hours in his logbook. Fun, outgoing guy, slated for a billet in a West Coast squadron of F9F-2 Panther jets.

Since all flights were solo, McBride, on his first flight leaped off with the typical wing wobble generated by most pilots unaccustomed to the boosted ailerons, and he was followed by his instructor in a chase plane, another TO-1. I was manning the radio at the landing end of the runway where we always stationed an instructor during flight ops. It was sort of a poor man's LSO (Landing Signal Officer) position; an instructor there to talk in the newer students as necessary during landings.

At the end of McBride's first flight, he reported in at 1,500 feet over our designated IP (Initial Position), a geographical fix about eight miles east of Whiting Field. Moments later he called, "I've had a flame out." Then a few seconds later, "It will not air start. I'm coming in."

From the end of the runway I could see him gliding toward the field, but I didn't say a word to him because I didn't know what to say. On a different frequency I declared an emergency at the field, calling crash trucks and meatwagons to the alert. He was high and wide on the downwind leg. Fast, too. But he dropped his wheels at his 180 degree position and started a gentle left turn toward the duty runway. At the ninety degree position, I could see his flaps coming down as he continued on in. Not a word said. Mac leveled off in a straightaway of about 2,000 feet – a little high. The silence was eerie. First flight, dead stick approach, and then he was on "glide slope." I could not believe how quiet it was as he passed overhead. McBride's plane touched down gently some 1,000 feet down the runway and he coasted to the last taxiway where he turned off and stopped. Wonderfully done.

Our instructor corps of fifteen pilots joined Skipper "Red" O'Neil in lauding Lieutenant McBride for a super job. I even got credit from Skipper for my part in this drama. Lieutenant Commander O'Neil said, "Moore, thanks for keeping your mouth shut."

It took a while in the onset of the jet age for pilots and medicine men alike to learn the exigencies of flight physiology. We flew sick, we flew with colds, we flew with fevers, we believed we were indestructible unless we struck the ground very hard and blew up. It was an attitude born of ignorance.

On a cloudy, rainy morning at Whiting Field our operations officer, Lieutenant Bill Allen, decided we should send one plane aloft to evaluate the weather conditions related to whether or not we should get our students airborne. I got the flight and leaped off although I did truly have a bad cold, which, among other things, tends to mess up the oxygen mask. No matter.

After roaring around the area at 30,000 feet, I declared the weather acceptable for flight ops and started down. Passing through 20,000 feet, the pressure in my ears turned to pain. I could not clear my ears by swallowing or valsalvalizing. At 15,000 feet, the pain was acute so I climbed back to 18,000 feet but was unable to clear my ears or relieve the pain. It sounds stupid but I even thought of bailing out, the pain was so severe. Fortunately, somewhere in flight training I learned that what goes up must come down and a glance at the fuel gage told me clearly that it was time to go down, but better in the airplane than in a parachute.

I radioed my dilemma and was to be greeted by a medic and a meatwagon since no one knew what to expect. At about 10,000 feet, all the pain suddenly abated. There was a bit of dizziness but no pain. It was a simple solution: My ear drums just blew out. The landing was uneventful. There was some blood and stuff in my helmet and I did not hear very well but well enough to understand the medic's instructions. So it was into the meatwagon for the trip to the NAS Pensacola Main Hospital and treatment for otitis media – bilaterally.

Several days and lots of penicillin later, the ears were healing well but my hands and feet started to swell and a rash broke out all over my body. Our flight surgeon saw the physiological debacle and broke out laughing. "Moore," he said, "you are allergic to penicillin." Pretty funny, doc. The ears healed but the swelling and rash lasted three miserable weeks.

From that I learned several things: (1) Don't fly with a cold; (2) if overseas and something unseemly happens ashore on liberty, take any medication except penicillin (the cure could be worse than the affliction); and (3) better still, don't do anything unseemly.

I had been aboard less than two months when the summons came from the Skipper's office (just call me "Red"). As every young aviator knows – Navy, Air Force, Marine, Coast Guard, Army, et al. – a call to the Skipper's office generally portends trouble. This turned out to be no exception.

"Moore," sez Red, "you are as of now our Ground Training Officer. I want you to formalize our syllabus, do something about the lousy classrooms we are using, and report back to me in one week with your plan."

How do you say "no thanks" to that? First thing I did after having given lectures in our small but adequate 20 by 50 foot classroom with internal temperatures hovering around 95 degrees was find some air conditioning for our schoolroom. I located two massive A/C units at Corey Field, which were not in use and had them hauled to Whiting Field and installed in our minuscule classroom. The installers cut huge holes in the wall for the installation, but it was done. A minor problem resulted. With the A/C units on, the room temperature was in the low 60s but the noise was so obtrusive the students could not hear the instructors.

It was back to Red O'Neil's office by invitation. "Moore, what's with the noise from the air conditioners? Fix it." That man could delegate.

So in the mini classroom with temperatures in the 60s and noise levels in excess of 120 decibels, I had installed a public address system with enough energy to drown out the air conditioners. All of this in a little bitty classroom in the hot months of northern Florida. Although it worked, it probably prolonged my livelihood as a lieutenant junior grade for several years before anyone would consider adding another bar to my collar.

Another gambit I employed turned out to be brilliant beyond my years. I listened in to all the lectures our instructors gave in the ground school curriculum and decided, with my vast several months' experience as head man in the ground school curriculum, that for the most part, the presentations were the pits. So I had the instructors record their lectures so we could listen to them played back for a learning venture. It was a marvelous instructional tool for all, including "moi," for we could hear how good and bad we truly were. With the recording device turned on for every lecture, the presentations improved markedly, and in fact the egos of all were triggered to the extent that ground school lecturers enjoyed listening to their messages to the classes as recorded on our el-cheapo machine ... and it was cool in there.

So Red surveyed the whole thing. He gave me an A in cool, a D- in noise, a C in public address system, and an overall B- in ground school administration. Can't make Admiral that way.

Some wonderfully dynamic and capable Navy and Marine pilots passed through the JTU gates at Whiting Field, a number of whom contributed to American history in general and Naval aviation lore in particular as the years passed – among them the following:

Lieutenant (j.g.) **Tom Hayward**.

I believe most of our students in the Jet Training Unit agreed that in time Tom would become Chief of Naval Operations. In 1978, he did. Tom and I became close friends and roommates aboard the carriers *Essex* and *Valley Forge* during the Korean thing. We later joined up at the Naval Air Test Center, both flying out of the Flight Test Division at Patuxent River, Maryland. A family man, a people man, an extraordinary leader of men and women in the Naval service. In the annals of Naval history, there have been none better.

Lieutenant (j.g.) **Bob Rostine**.

He played the dynamics of flying as Isaac Stern plays the violin. He made every airplane he ever flew look good. Chance Vought Aircraft hired him as their premier test pilot and project pilot on the F8U Crusader and then the A7 Intruder. Bob served as chief test pilot for Vought for a number of years before climbing out of the cockpit for good. A few years after Rostine's flying days ended, he succumbed to cancer, which seemed like an inglorious and unfair way for such an achiever to go.

Commander Marshall Beebe.

I had Marsh as a student at JTU – Lieutenant (j.g.) Moore instructing Commander Beebe in the art of flying jets. He was so good and his presence so strong that I felt intimidated twenty-four hours a day for his month at JTU. Beebe was Commander of Air Group Five flying out of NAS North Island, San Diego, and was kind enough to drag Rostine and me along to Korea in his air group. A double ace in WW II, we used to kid about his having shot down fourteen airplanes, many of which were the enemy. (Behind his back, of course.) Commander Beebe was a dynamic tiger, forever regarded with reverence by Naval aviation. I had the privilege of flying with Marsh when he became Director of the Flight Test Division, Patuxent River. At the onset of the Flexdeck Program (See Pax Riv.), I was ordered to England to fly in the British flexdeck program and was accompanied by Commander Beebe. He wasn't about to be left out. He made it look easy. It wasn't. Marsh Beebe passed away a few years ago. He had lived life fully and well. Marsh was immortalized by James Michener in *The Bridges of Toko-Ri* which was dedicated to him. He will not be forgotten.

J. Lynn Helms.

Lynn was an instructor in JTU, one of ten on board when I joined up. Intelligent, articulate, quick – Lynn as a first lieutenant in the Marines, made the Corps look good in the air. On the ground, Lynn always had an answer. He wasn't always right but was right often enough that we believed almost everything he said. After JTU he chased MIG-15s in Air Force F-86s as an exchange pilot, then joined our cadre of Moore, Hayward, Rostine and Beebe at Flight Test, NATC. From there, Lynn's career went ever onward and upward – V.P. North American Aviation in Columbus; V.P. and Group Leader, Bendix; President, Hamilton Standard; President and CEO, Piper, and finally, Chief of the Federal Aviation Administration (FAA). Not bad for a little old first lieutenant.

Red and Mogi O'Neil.

Red, an intense, young Lieutenant Commander was commanding officer of JTU-1: an organizer, a disciplinarian, a leader. But what we all liked best about Red was his beautiful wife Mogi. What elegance. Mogi was/ is three-quarters Cherokee and Creek Indian. She had enough charm for a squadron of women, more than enough dark-haired, dark-eyed beauty to be a movie star. Mogi complemented Red's military achievements with her warmth and grace as if she were born to it.

Lieutenant Commander O'Neil retired as Captain V. P. O'Neil, USN, after having been Skipper of an F2H-2 Banshee squadron (VF-44); having graduated from the War College; having served a six-year sentence in the Pentagon; and a tour as Commander, the Naval Air Test Center, Patuxent River. Red and Mogi – what a pair they were and are – now cooling it in Key Largo, Florida.

Captain **Russ McJunkin**, USN (retired).

Russ was one of my very first students in the JTU syllabus. He was a bright-faced young Ensign with a great smile and all the enthusiasm of a Charles Lindbergh. For reasons I cannot recall, the two of us were followed by the news media and made the cover of at least one national magazine. Russ was photogenic and talented enough to have flown the Atlantic solo a la Lindbergh had the timing been right.

At the completion of his training tour at JTU, we attended "graduation" ceremonies at the Officers Club, which consisted of lots of joy and the downing of a few beers. The following day, Marilynn and I were relaxing on our front porch at home watching son Randy chase butterflies and pick sand spurs from his socks when up drove now jet pilot, Ensign McJunkin, with his mother and father in a celebratory mood. They had come for a short visit with Dad McJunkin carrying a case of very expensive wine, a gift from the three McJunkins. For me that had never happened before, or since. And then they were off.

Although I have not seen Russ since that afternoon forty-five years ago, I remember him with respect and gentleness. Pictures of the two of us released by the news media are this day on the walls of my family room along with other aviation memorabelia from years gone by. I have displayed only things which make me smile.

Capt. Russ McJunkin, USN, ret. now lives in the islands, in Tortola or St. Thomas or thereabouts, and runs an air charter service of some kind, so I'm told. I'd fly with him!

VII

KOREA I

When I received orders to the fleet from JTU, it was with exhilaration that I found I had been ordered to Air Group Five in San Diego. Fellow instructor Rip Rostine (as in Rip VanWinkle) also received orders to A.G. Five, commanded by Commander Marsh Beebe. As was noted before, Beebe had gone through our JTU syllabus, with flying colors I might add, and had arranged with the Navy's BuPers (Bureau of Personnel) for Rostine and me to receive orders to his Air Group scheduled to deploy in the fall of 1951 aboard USS *Essex*, CVA-9. And so it was that Rip and I found ourselves members of Lieutenant Commander Ernie Beauchamp's VF-51 team headed for Korea.

In our early training days with VF-51, we had everything but airplanes. Somehow our Skipper had scrounged up six F9F-2 Panthers, which we flew around-the-clock. VF-52, also flying F9F-2s had five Panthers in their inventory; theirs hangared with ours as we prepared for Korea. VF-52 was scheduled to depart with our Air Group but at the last minute was replaced by an F2H-1 Banshee squadron out of Jacksonville, Florida.

In the early training days, we needed all six of our Panthers up and available on a continuing basis. Parts were always a problem in the maintenance cycle, and as Maintenance Officer of our squadron, I found the logistics headaches to be as much of a pain as a Lieutenant (j.g.) could control with aspirin alone.

We found our Panthers being grounded because the tip tank fuel caps were breaking off in flight and we could not get replacement caps from the supply system or even directly from Grumman Iron Works. We had got down to two Panthers flyable when I'd had enough. I called our materiel chief, P.E. Hall, in for an official reaming and a stern admonition that I wanted fuel caps on those tip tanks within forty-eight hours or he was dead. I did not care where he got them, I told him; just get them. That was a mistake.

The very next morning every one of our six Panthers had tip tank caps, were ready to fly, and were soon airborne. Then the phone rang. It seemed that all of VF-52s Panthers were grounded. No tip tank caps. P. E. Hall was something else.

Our flight training program for the Korean thing was well under way in the summer of '51 with twenty-four pilots and a full complement of Panthers aboard, but not without some problems and some heartaches.

Our Skipper, Ernie Beauchamp, continually emphasized discipline in our flight operations, which included being sharp and looking good around the airfield or the ship. True enough, the only part of our flight performance apparent to the the ship's crew was how we looked when we rendezvoused after launch and how we looked when we returned from a mission.

At NAS North Island in San Diego where we were based and trained for our initial assault against the North Korean gang, we flew tactical exercises over Southern California, intercept missions against Air Force attack airplanes, and other exercises designed to hone our skills as we prepared to defend our motherland against the North Korean enemy.

When we returned to NAS North Island, we stringently acceded to our Skipper's wishes that we look as good as the Navy's Blue Angels flight demonstration team when we flew over the field in echelon for our break-up overhead into the landing pattern. Skipper most often ventured outside as one of our flight divisions approached to be assured we looked good overhead in our landing approach. That wasn't his desire – it was an order.

On this day, the division I was part of was led by aviator extraordinaire Dick Wenzell. We had been practicing tactics against make-believe MIG 15s, which would have whipped our F9F-2 butts in a moment, but undaunted, we would go down in flames with elan. So we returned to North Island after our exercise, elegant in our right-echelon as we approached the duty runway at North Island. Skipper would be watching. Wenzell's wingman was Bud Gardner. I was the section leader and my wingman was Neil Armstrong. Indeed, we looked great as we flew over the field at 1,500 feet, 250 knots.

At the break, Wenzell looked at Gardner, saluted, then broke hard left into a 90-degree bank away from the echelon. Five seconds later, as planned, Bud saluted me, then broke hard left into a 90-degree bank, but his plane immediately went upside-down and nose down. It was extraordinarily startling to watch from my vantage point. Bud rolled his plane upright but was angled toward the ground at about 60 degrees. It was over in an instant. His plane impacted the ground to the left side of the runway, precipitating a huge, ugly explosion with a dark red and black fireball, the usual colors of airplanes exploding upon impact with the ground – hues signaling the end of an airplane and often the death of its pilot.

The three of us circled the field as the crash trucks raced to the morbid scene until we were allowed to land on the same runway alongside which was the burning wreckage of Bud's plane.

The ready room was somber as one might surmise. We had lost a fine young pilot preparing for combat and questions permeated the gathering of pilots. Bud had apparently snap rolled his Panther and lost his life as a consequence. But why? And how?

Two days later Dick Wenzell and I took off in our F9F-2s to find some answers. We surmised that Bud had rolled sharply to his left into a 90-degree bank, which I saw, then pulled back hard on the stick to effect a turn, but that in itself wouldn't do it. He must have kicked hard left rudder as well, we believed, otherwise he would not have ended upside-down.

Wenzell and I leveled off at 10,000 feet and I backed away about 100 yards while Dick, as programmed, tried to duplicate the maneuver which killed Bud Gardner. Dick steadied at 250 knots, threw in hard left stick, pulled back sharply, and threw in left rudder. The Panther snap rolled inverted with Dick applying corrective controls as Bud had tried to do. It took Wenzell 4,000 feet to recover. Bud had only 1,500 feet.

I repeated the maneuver several times as did Wenzell, each time with the same results. Hard left rudder snap rolled the Panther – which was okay at 10,000 feet but fatal at 1,500 feet. It all seemed so strange to us since we seldom used the rudders in single-engine jets except for braking and turning on the ground. The brakes were located on the rudder pedals. In flight you could keep your shoes in a tote bag awaiting a landing of some kind when braking the airplane was in order.

Bud's death was tragic for us as we prepared for the Korean adventure. Unfortunately, it would not be our last loss in our assignment to defend America's honor against the North Korean aggressors in the Communist world about which most of us knew very little.

On August 21, 1951, I was introduced to combat over North Korea where the guys down below were shooting real live bullets at us. Those bastards were trying to kill us! Our Carrier, *Essex*, CVA-9, had joined Task Force 77 about forty miles off the Korean coast the day before and it all began for me and my squadronmates the very cool morning of Augusttwenty-first.

There were a lot of veterans in Air Group 5 aboard *Essex*. We had a squadron of F4U Corsairs, one of AD Skyraiders, one of F2H-1 Banshees, and our own squadron, VF-51, flying F9F-2s plus a photo detachment also flying Panthers.

Every pilot remembers his or her first combat mission, remembers the anxiety, the fear, the uncertainties, the excitement – yes, the excitement. And so to share with those whose airplanes have been shot at and also those who have not been so exposed, I offer candid impressions of my introduction to combat in an F9F-2 Panther as I flew a nervous tail end Charlie in a division of four planes led by Lieutenant John Scott. This was his second tour and who better to lead the way. As for myself, I did not do well.

Immediately after this mission I had dictated my recollections of the event into a taperecorder. The following is based on a transcript of those memories:

More than once I asked myself, "John, just what are you doing out here? You should be home instructing students to fly, or supporting the bar at the Pensacola 'O' Club. You're no hero, boy, let's face it."

When the alarm went off at 0300, I wasn't rudely awakened because I'd hardly slept. The night before, Lieutenant John Scott's division of four jets had been scheduled for an early-morning strike on a supply dump just south of Wonsan. All night long, I had rolled and tossed and slept fitfully, tormented by thoughts of my baptism by fire in the morning.

I ate breakfast at 0330 because everyone else ate breakfast. I wasn't hungry. The briefing in the ready room was well organized by Ensign Ken Danneberg, our Intelligence Officer. Weather over the target was good and aerology reported only a few scattered clouds around the force. We were starboard carrier, so our flight was briefed to rendezvous on the starboard side at 1,500 feet, outside the screen of protecting destroyers.

"Here's the flak chart giving all known gun positions in your area," said Danneberg.

I wondered if there were a chance I might be grounded at the last minute. I could go on sick call. I felt guilty for even thinking such thoughts.

But I consoled myself with the thought that a lot of other pilots who had done a fine job out here were probably just as scared and nervous as I about their first hop. I had trained for this a long time and I was going to go through with it even if it killed me. Right there my reasoning got a little weak.

I took the photos of the target that Ken had given me and put them in my map folder along with a batch of charts of Wonsan and the rest of Korea. If I ever got lost over Korea it wouldn't be the surveyor's fault.

After the briefing was over I started struggling into my vast collection of flight paraphernalia designed to keep me alive in the event of almost any emergency. The water temperature was in the forties; I wore a very remarkable exposure suit, which would keep me dry as a bone if I ended up in the water. They might have trouble finding me in the water; I carried flares, flashlights and a whistle. Sharks might bother me; I had shark repellent. I might get hungry; I had fishing gear. In case I should get shot down over land, I might have to shoot it out with the Commies; I had a .38 revolver and seventy-five rounds of ammo. Might have to cut my way through underbrush; I had three knives. The drinking water would be contaminated; I had Halazone tablets, and if that wasn't enough, the aureomycin, terramycin and APC tablets would cure anything else. Might run across some friendly natives and want to talk to them; a handy little pointy-talky book fitted neatly in my trouser leg. Might cut myself; I had a first aid kit. Might want to travel across land to reach friendly troops; a map and two compasses would solve the navigation problem. Then for other emergencies an extra pair of socks, underdrawers, cigarettes, vitamin pills, signal mirror, all might come in handy. When the other pilots called me "Task Force Moore," I smiled with an air of confidence.

I zipped up my poofy bag (exposure suit). If I went down in the water, I probably wouldn't freeze to death for half-an-hour, maybe even three-quarters of an hour. If I weren't wearing this suit I could freeze to death rather quickly. But I knew if I went into the drink, our helicopters would have me out in no time at all. They were good at it. They had rescued lots of pilots. Yeah, they'd get me out. I knew they would. I hoped.

"All ready rooms from Air Ops: Pilots, man your planes."

It was 0515. I grabbed my maps and kneepad and went topside to the flight deck. It was dark as pitch. The task force hadn't turned into the wind as yet, but a twenty knot wind was blowing across the flight deck and it was cold. I finally found my plane aft of the No. 2 elevator on the port side. Specks of light in the east gave an indication the sun would rise as it was expected to do. I guess for a lot of people in the world, this was just another day. But for me, it wasn't starting out like any day I had ever known. Our main objective at sunrise was being around to see sunset.

Kilgore, my very capable plane captain, had pre-flight checked the plane and was waiting for me. He took my map case and kneepad to stow them in the cockpit while I checked over the plane.

"Where's your helmet, Mr. Moore?" he asked. I'd forgotten the damn thing. I told Kilgore where I'd left it in the ready room and he got it for me.

There were some odds and ends to take care of in the cockpit, like climbing into my 'chute, plugging in the G-suit and the bail-out bottle, hooking up the life raft lanyard, hooking up radio transmitter and receiver cords, fastening shoulder straps to the safety belt, then pulling them up tight. As some Air Force jockey in Korea said, "I don't get into my jet. I strap it on."

Then came two helmets to be put on, and three pair of gloves: nylon first, then rubber gloves, then leather ones on the outside of the other two. If a pilot has any bug bites or a rash that has to be scratched, he's got to get all his scratching done before he gets buckled into his plane; otherwise, he has to wait 'til he gets back to do it. Makes it kind of hard on the athletes. If it hadn't been for Kilgore, I'd never have been ready.

The word was passed to start the prop planes so their engines could warm up . . . I was still getting my plane strapped on. I kept glancing hopefully toward the east as if trying to hurry the sunrise.

"Stand by to start the jets," came the word over the bullhorn from primary fly. In less than an hour, I was going to be shot at. This was stuff for heroes, not for average men.

I knew I couldn't go over there and win this war by myself. We all knew that. But we all felt that if we could maybe knock out a supply dump, it would mean just that much less stuff getting to the Commie front lines to support their troops. If we could blow up an ammo dump, there would be that much less ammo for them to shoot at our boys in the front lines. The Navy interdiction program was very sound and we all believed in it.

They got a starting unit hooked up to my plane, and in a minute or two the engine was idling smoothly.

The task force turned into the wind and a chilly cutting forty knots of of autumn air blew down the flight deck. At 0545, the words "white flag" came over the bullhorn, and up in primary fly, an arm came out of a cracked window, withdrew a red flag mounted there, and replaced it with a white flag, which fluttered viciously in the gale. The arm withdrew very quickly and the window slammed shut.

This was it!

The first jet was catapulted into the early morning sunrise. There were twenty jets on this launch from our ship: four flying combat air patrol and the other sixteen hitting assigned targets over North Korea. The four of us in John Scott's division were carrying eight 250-pound bombs each. We thought we were very formidable.

"Steady, John, don't be so nervous," I said to myself. " Just watch the taxi signalman and you'll be okay. The taxi signalman over there, you idiot."

I'd been watching an ordnanceman. They're pretty hard to tell apart: the ordnanceman is wearing a bright red jersey and red helmet, and the taxi signalman a bright yellow jersey and yellow helmet. Oh well, we all make mistakes.

Collecting my wits, I spread my wings, dropped my flaps, and went over the check-off list. The seasoned flight deck crew maneuvered me onto the starboard catapult I had full power on and gave the signal to the catapult officer that I was ready to go. The catapult doesn't launch you, it sort of throws you into the air. One instant the plane is sitting still, then the catapult is fired. In less than two seconds, the plane is flying along at better than 120 knots. (The *Essex* had two H4B hydraulic catapults)

I swished down the catapult thinking, "They can't do this to me!" Here I was airborne on my first combat mission in S-106, one of our newest Panther jets.

I closed my canopy and although the plane was slow to accelerate, I brought up my flaps. I was in a mild state of shock, it seemed. I turned to the starboard and passed over the screen. The plane seemed to be very slow picking up speed. Tachometer said 100 percent power. Suddenly, another Panther streaked by and I heard in my earphones, "S106, pull up your wheels." I knew I'd forgotten something.

By the time I got up to rendezvous altitude, I could see the other three planes in our flight two o'clock from me, about three miles away. They were joined up and waiting for old slow poke. I closed on them, checked side numbers on the planes to make sure I had the right flight, then called on the radio, "John One, this is John Four, all aboard."

Scott checked us in with Crabapple, ship's call, and we switched to a tactical radio frequency and headed for the beach. There was a pronounced sinking feeling in my stomach as I saw the fleet disappear aft of my tail section.

It was a magnificent morning. I admired all the beautiful red and orange colors of the sunrise. And here I was going out to get my butt shot off when I should have been at home, snuggled down in the Beautyrest, helping the electric blanket keep Marilynn warm.

We leveled off at 16,000 feet. Ahead, the coast of North Korea loomed out of the sea. I was a little disappointed at seeing it for the first time. It looked just like the coast of New England or some places in California. Guess I'd expected to see rolling hills protected by continuous bursts of anti-air-craft fire with planes crashing into the sea all around and tanks dueling in the fields.

We crossed over Wonsan Bay. The peaceful appearance of the rug-ged countryside ahead was deceptive. Although you couldn't see them, I knew the land down there was infested with anti-aircraft guns; each one manned by gunners who had been shooting at Navy planes for more than a year.

"John Flight from John One, count off," came Scotty's voice over the radio.

"John Two to John Three." That was Freddie Evans.

"John Three to John Four." That was Rip Rostine.

"John Four back to One." That was me.

As we turned south about five miles west of Wonsan, our division leader wanted to be sure all our radios were working before we tangled with the Red gunners over our target.

In the cockpit, I was camouflaged by maps and charts. One map had taken me to Wonsan Harbor. I folded it like a "Dear John" letter and stuffed it in the corner of the cockpit. No time for neatness now. Another map was a blow-up of the Wonsan area. It showed Wonsan, Kowan to the north, Anbyon to the south down Death Valley where we were going. I stuffed it in the corner. A third map was a blow-up of our immediate target area south of Wonsan. I traced down the river with my finger, looked out of the cockpit at the river below. It matched the map exactly.

Just south of a large bend in the river, the map showed a road head-ing up into the hills. Our target was a group of supply buildings about a half mile up that road. There it was down below, bigger than life.

The McDonell FH-1 Phantom.

A Lockheed TO-1 (F-80) Shooting Star of JTU-1, NAS Whiting Field, FL.

Instructor, Lt. (j.g.). John Moore, (right) and student Ens. Russ McJunkin at Whiting in the Fall of 1949.

Midshipman Neil Armstrong of VF-51 on the beach near Barber's Point NAS, Hawaii, in 1951. Following his Navy career, Armstrong would be the first man on the moon.

A frozen John Moore on the flight deck of aircraft carrier *Valley Forge* in the Sea of Japan, off the coast of Korea in 1953.

The air group of *Valley Forge* is grounded by a storm off Korea.

A Grumman F9F-5 Panther of VF-51.

Sugar 115 of VF-51 comes out of the arresting gear as the pilot begins to fold the Panther's wings.

VF-51's "Rip" Rostine returns from a mission over North Korea.

A sequence of ten photos on this and next page records the last "wheels up" landing in the Navy Flexdeck program at Pax River NAS. The aircraft is a Grumman F9F-7 and the pilot is John Moor

The author tries out the special Flexdeck retenti[on] harness.

Lt. John Moore at Patuxent NAS, MD in 1954,

An aerial view of the rubberized Flexdeck alongside Runway 13 at Pax River.

Pilot John Moore and Engineer Lt. Don Heile chat on the Pax River flight test
ramp while preparing for the steam catapult tests.

A Vought F7U-3 piloted by Floyd Nugent is "shot" from the deck of *Hancock* during Project
Steam. Nugent later ejected from this aircraft.

Above: Author has just landed and hooked the third wire of *Shangri-La's* arresting gear during initial carrier trials of the F7U-3M Cutlass; and below the arresting gear has extended to the "end of run-out."

John Moore was also pilot for carrier trials of the Douglas AD-5N Skyraider, shown here about to be catapulted.

It seemed uncanny. How in the hell did this topographer know exactly how the road curved up into the mountains?

Across the road from our target, the map pictured a small pear-shaped village of perhaps one hundred buildings. There it was down below, exactly as depicted.

A large ugly ball of fire dissolved into a black cloud off my port wing tip. Then another. Then three more. It was scary.

"Scotty, they're shooting at us," I yelled. I forgot to push the mike button.

"John! John! They're shooting at us," I yelled, holding the mike button down with all five thumbs on my left hand.

"Roger," spoke John One.

We were at 12,000 feet now in a port turn, doing 410 knots. We'd been briefed to make a high speed run-in, drop two bombs in the first attack to the northeast, then make a right-hand recovery to the south. That would take us away from an angry pack of automatic weapons just north of the target.

The black puffs were above and slightly aft of John One now. But so was I. Disturbing coincidence.

"This is John One. Dive brakes."

I dropped my dive brakes as the target came into my gunsight. Didn't want our speed to build up too high – makes it too hard to stay on the target. Small white puffs replaced the black ones and the sky was full of them – 37s or 40 mm. It was barrage fire. We plowed right through it: 6,000 feet ... 5,000 feet ... 4,000 feet ... 3,500 feet. I pushed the bomb pickle and pulled hard on the stick, bringing up my dive brakes. The oxygen mask pulled on my cheeks. My head sagged between my shoulders. It was difficult to see for a moment – partial gray-out. I'd pulled 6.5 G. Tracers crossed in front of my nose. I made a hard right turn. Up ahead John One, Two and Three were jinking to throw off the Commie gunners.

I looked back and saw six clouds of black smoke rising from the target. Good hits. How come only six? Should be eight. "Some knucklehead forgot to turn on his bomb selector switches," I said to myself – then glanced at mine. They were off. Damn! How could I be so stupid? Come all the way over here to help win this war, fly through clouds of flak, then didn't drop any bombs because I forgot to turn on my switches. I felt stupid.

John Four, check bomb switches." I knew the voice. "How did he know it was me?"

We hit again to the south after climbing to 9,000 feet. This time more tracers than before. I pickled off four bombs then pulled out and broke hard starboard. The black clouds from our bombs were rising. All bombs hit in the target except two. Two little black clouds were growing several hundred feet north of the target on a mountain slope. I'd put two bombs in and two over the supply building. "Not bad," I thought. I was amazed that I'd hit anything at all. Although I hadn't demolished an atomic energy factory or a tremendous manufacturing area, I felt pretty good about getting two good hits with my first four bombs.

As we rolled in for a third attack the radio spoke: "This is John One. This time recover to port. We'll make the next run to the southeast. Three acknowledge. Over."

"John Three, Roger."

Guess he felt the anti-aircraft fire couldn't be any worse to the west of the target than what we'd seen to the east. Besides, the diversion might throw them off. Bomb switches on. A nasty black burst off my starboard wing. I felt that one. We were steep on this run. Sixty mils looked like a good lead. Thirty-five hundred feet – pickle. I pulled hard on the stick. The ground turned gray. Then the sky, It was gray too. Six G pull-out. The G suit pressed hard on my abdomen ... gray-out but no black-out. Tracers coming up at one o'clock reminded me to break hard port.

I had 100 percent power on and cut inside John Three. White puffs formed at four o'clock down. They were way off this time. I wasn't so scared now, but apprehensive as all get out. All eyeballs. One more bombing run then probably a strafing run. I knew Scott was aching to shoot up some of the anti-aircraft positions. You could see them blinking away in tiny holes like flies. But our target was the supply depot. We'd get the AA positions another day. A good fire had started on the eastern end of the target. Looked like four of the five buildings were burning.

John Two rolled over on his back behind John One, pulled through until he got on the target, then rolled out. More tracers. Those tracers sure are distracting in a bombing run. I saw Scott's bombs go off. Right on target. It was a mess. I pickled off my last two bombs and pulled back. Then ... Blooey! Felt like someone had hit my plane with a sledgehammer.

"John One. I'm hit! I'm hit!"

"Roger. Three, get behind Four and check his plane," came our division leader's voice loud and clear. Fortunately, Scotty knew my voice over the radio because I'd failed to identify myself. Already Rostine had dropped his dive brake and was falling back on my port side. I was climbing and heading northeast toward the water.

"John Four from One. How bad are you hit? Can you control it? Over."

I tried the controls. I checked the engine instruments. I checked the gauges. There was nothing abnormal. Then I rocked the wings and looked out at my ailerons. There it was. A jagged hole was torn in my port wing about a foot inboard the tip tank. It appeared to be at least eighteen inches in length but not too wide. The controls felt solid.

I called John. "One from Four. I think I'll be okay. I've got a hole outboard in my port wing. Looks like it might have been a 20 mm. Over."

"Roger. This is John One. We'll be over water in a couple of minutes. Hold your heading. We'll join up on you. Over."

"Four. Roger," I replied.

I unpuckered. The adrenalin moved over and made room for some blood to flow through my veins. "Settle down," I told myself. "You're all right."

The coastline of Korea passed under my wing as I climbed through 10,000 feet, so I took a heading down the coast toward friendly South Korea – just in case. To be on the safe side, John Scott had notified Air Sea Rescue. They'd have helicopters warming up, ready to go if things took a turn for the worse.

"John from Four. I'm going to stall check my plane. I think I can get her back aboard okay. Over."

"John One, Roger."

The formation moved out to the side behind me. I was at 14,000 feet now. Dive brakes slowed me to 200 knots and I dropped my wheels and flaps. Seventy percent power. One hundred fifty knots ... 130 ... 120 ... 110 ... the stick-shaker stall-warning device cut in, warning of an impending stall. The left wing was getting heavy. Took right rudder and aileron to compensate for the drag set up by that jagged hole in the port wing. She shuddered and almost stalled at 104 knots. I eased the nose over, added throttle, leveled my wings, brought up my wheels and watched my speed build up. At 135 knots, I brought up the flaps.

"John One from Four. I can get aboard."

"Roger. This is One. Join up. Switch to channel white."

We closed on our leader and moved into a cruising formation as we headed for the task force. John gave us a signal to check ordnance switches, make sure they were off and guns on safe. I checked my switches and notified John Three by visual signal that I had done so, then added a few obscene signals as a sign of affection. It was a ritual in our division.

In a short time, I heard Scott's voice again. "Hello, Crabapple, this is One Zero Two Crabapple. See you ahead thirty miles. Over."

"This is Crabapple. Roger. Give me a call when you are overhead. Over."

"This is One Zero Two Crabapple. Roger. Out."

I still couldn't see the ships in the force. Although the visibility was good, the early morning light made it difficult to pick them up. Finally, there they were. Tiny specks on the water.

Soon we were over the fleet. "Hello, Crabapple, this is One Zero Two Crabapple. Over you with four F9Fs, angels fourteen. No hung ordnance. One plane battle damaged. Side number Sugar One Zero Six. Over."

"This is Crabapple. Roger. Can Sugar One Zero Six stay airborne until Charlie time? Over."

The admiral would turn the task force into the wind right now to land us aboard if it were an emergency but he'd prefer not to bring us in until scheduled landing time which was ten minutes away.

"This is One Zero Two Crabapple. Affirmative. He can make scheduled Charlie. Out."

An awful lot had happened since 0545 – an hour and twenty minutes ago. I had almost completely recovered from my introduction to combat. I was beginning to feel proud. "You got some good hits on those supply buildings," I told myself. "Maybe you're the one who started the fire. Now all you've got to do is land aboard that postage stamp down there with a hole in your wing."

The *Essex*, a straight deck carrier, looked to be about a half-inch long and a sixteenth-of-an-inch wide from 14,000 feet. Not much to land a jet on. Fortunately, it got a little larger when I got around to landing on it.

As we orbited the ship awaiting our signal to descend and land, I realized I'd matured several years in that last hour and a half and it was a good feeling. I'd be left-wing heavy when I brought her aboard, I knew, so I'd have to make my approach wider and come in a little faster.

Below the tiny snails were turning to the starboard, all turning at the same time and each one leaving a curved white trail behind. They make a beautiful pattern.

"Hello, One Zero Two Crabapple, your signal is Charlie."

At a sign from John One, we dropped our dive brakes and started down. We passed over our helicopter, which was hovering low over the water on the *Essex*'s starboard quarter waiting like a guardian angel to help out a pilot who might have trouble and have to ditch during landing operations. In a close starboard echelon, we flew low past our floating home. Scotty broke off to enter the landing pattern, followed by Fred and Rip at about fifteen second intervals. I watched Rostine after he broke off, so I could get a little longer interval than usual for our landing. I broke and dropped my wheels. I was still a little nervous from recent events but a nervous man instead of a nervous boy. On the downwind leg, I was still going like a bat out of hell – couldn't get slowed down.

Check-off list, you stupe, I reminded myself. Go over your landing check-off list! Hook down ... check. Wheels down and locked ... check. Flaps down ... Damn! I'd forgotten them. I dropped my flaps and immediately began slowing up. I was going to be too fast when I started my turn into the final approach. I wanted 120 knots as I rolled into my approach turn. I had 150 knots. I eased the stick over to the left to start my turn. I finally got my speed down to 120 knots, as I picked up the landing signal officer in the groove. He was about a quarter inch high some thousand yards away.

He was holding a high signal on me when I picked him up, so I eased my nose over. If a pilot coming around for a landing will put the ship's uppermost antenna just a little above the horizon, his altitude above the flight deck will be about right for the approach. I set my altitude up thusly and the LSO dropped his high signal down to a "Roger" – a signal paddle in each hand held out horizontally, signifying to the pilot to keep it coming just as it is, that everything is okay. Then I got a slant signal. I steepened my turn a little more. Then another high. I eased the nose over again. Then a fast. I took off some throttle. A low. I'd lost too much altitude. Now another slant, a low dip, a slow, and a wave-off. I poured on the power, turned to the left and passed about twenty feet over the port side of the flight deck. "What a lousy approach," I told myself, reflecting no doubt the exact thoughts of the LSO, the air officer, and the squadron commander. How can one person do so many things so poorly by 0715 in the morning? I really buckled down then. I was tired of being stupid. I was a combat pilot who'd been out destroying enemy supplies, and I was proud of that. I knew I'd been nervous and scared on this hop, and as a result had done some dumb things. I had a fairly good record in training and although stupidity wasn't too much out of the ordinary for me, this was excessive to put it mildly. Damn it!

Another division of our planes was coming up the starboard side of the ship to break for landing. I was ahead of them so I turned port to come around for another approach. The LSO picked me up with a "Roger." Altitude and speed were right on ... 115 knots. A slant signal increased my turn to keep from over shooting the groove. Now I was lined up with the center of the flight deck. A high. I eased the nose over slightly. Now a "Roger." Now another high. I must have climbed a little. I eased the nose over again and rolled in some forward trim tab. A "Roger." Then a cut. I pulled the throttle back to idle, eased the nose over – the flight deck was coming up fast. Back stick to cushion the landing. I lurched forward against the snug shoulder harness as my tailhook engaged an arresting cable on the flight deck. From 110 knots to a standstill in 130 feet. I rolled backward a short distance and retracted my tailhook. The yellow-shirted taxi signalman waved frantically for me to add power and move forward of the landing area to make room for another jet now turning into the groove. Forward another yellow-shirt had me fold my wings. Then he held his gloved hands in front of him and opened and closed them like jaws of a barking dog. I brought my flaps up. I was being parked on the port side between the planes Fred and Rip had flown. Rip, out of his plane, waved as he passed under my wing on the way aft to the ready room. He was all smiles. Hold brakes, cut engine, yellow-shirt signaled.

Kilgore climbed up the side of my plane and stuck his head inside the cockpit.

"How'd it go, Mr. Moore?" he greeted me.

"Fine," I said nonchalantly. Combat veteran.

The ordnancemen were unloading the 20 mm cannon in the nose of my plane. I hadn't gotten around to firing them. Kilgore helped me with the maze of straps and wires which bound me to my steed. I gathered the wrinkled maps up from the corner of the cockpit and made an attempt to fold them neatly. Didn't want any razzing about how they got so battered.

"What did you run into, Mr. Moore?" Chief Waldon asked, smiling from ear to ear. He was on his second Korean combat tour. He'd patched lots of flak holes.

"Must have made somebody mad over there," I answered, smiling as I walked past him.

Clutching my maps, I let the cold wind push me down the deck toward the entrance to our ready room. Another jet landed aboard. Waddling clumsily down the deck in my poofy bag, I felt good. I didn't think of the bombs I'd dropped which hit up on the mountainside, but my bombs which hit the target were vivid in my mind. I didn't think of the flak either. All I could think of was blowing up the enemy's supplies. I felt like part of a darned good team. No flag-waving, either. In my own hair-raising way, I had helped a good cause.

As I jumped onto the catwalk and ducked into a passageway, I thought, "Maybe the next time you'll use your head a little more."

I walked into the ready room.

"The returning hero! How'd it go, John?" asked Ken Danneberg.

"No strain. Nothing to it." I replied.

In the spring of 1951, a bright young blond-headed kid joined our squadron as we prepared for our first mission to Korea. It was VF-51's second mission. The kid's name was Neil Armstrong and he wasn't even an Ensign. He had won his Navy Wings of Gold and been designated an Ensign, but because of a paperwork foul-up, his commission had not come through the pipeline and he was Midshipman Armstrong, flying F9F-2s preparing to go to war.

I had the good fortune to fly a lot with Neil. He couldn't have been more than twenty-two years old, but he was mature in flying skills with intellect beyond his years. And he was refreshingly curious. Our Skipper, Lieutenant Commander Ernie Beauchamp, recognized these desirable traits in Neil and assigned him to the billet of Safety Officer, responsible for pilot safety equipment and related procedures oriented toward keeping our squadron pilots alive throughout the upcoming Korean venture.

In a four-week period during which we took our squadron lock-stock-and-barrel over the mountains to NAS El Centro from NAS North Island for gunnery and bombing training the unmistakable evidence of Armstrong's intensity became manifest. The Navy's principal parachute training school was located at El Centro only a short jeep ride from our squadron's location on the field. Neil requested permission from our CO to visit the school to enhance his knowledge of parachutes and related personal equipment. Skipper acquiesced with an admonition to be careful – we could not afford to have anyone injured as we approached departure date for Korea. "We need all our pilots, trained and healthy, ready to go on schedule," Beauchamp said over and over throughout training. Neil said he would be careful.

Two days later, Armstrong was scheduled to brief all our pilots about his learning experience at the parachute school. Neil gave an articulate account of parachute packing procedures, the importance of properly fitted leg and shoulder harnesses, the importance of instinctively knowing the rip-cord "D" ring location, how best to separate from the ejection seat, and what to expect physiologically when the parachute opened. It was during his explanation of how to land with knees bent and roll on the ground with the drift that the stuff hit the fan.

Lieutenant Commander Beauchamp wanted to know how he knew all this stuff and Neil said, "Sir, because I did it."

Skipper was livid. "You mean that you risked injury by making a parachute jump when I distinctly told you to be careful and not get hurt?" Beauchamp yelled at Midshipman Armstrong. None of us had ever seen Ernie so pissed.

"But, Sir," said the Midshipman, "I was careful."

It took a while for Beauchamp to cool it and digest what Neil had done. An hour or so later, I was in his office on an airplane maintenance matter and even as I sat down, Beauchamp smiled and said to me, "That kid is something else, isn't he?"

It was ironic that the experience Neil gained in his controlled parachute jump at the school would be most helpful to him some months later in combat.

Enroute to Japan from Hawaii on the USS *Essex*, CVA-9, we had an evening briefing in our readyroom, and at muster everyone showed up except our Midshipman. No one knew where he was. Then one of his roommates (junior officer bunkroom) reported that he might be in one of the crew lounges teaching class. "What class?" asked Beauchamp. No one knew of it, but Armstrong was teaching algebra to "his" class of about thirty sailors three nights a week in crew quarters. A phone call from our ready room duty officer instigated a call on the ship's PA system, "Midshipman Armstrong, please report to your readyroom." Minutes later the Midshipman burst into the rear door of readyroom No. 2, apologizing for being late. "No excuses, Sir." There would be no excuses.

Beauchamp: "Neil, where were you?"

"Down below, Sir."

"What were you doing down below?"

"Sir," said Armstrong, as if apologizing, "I am teaching an algebra class to some of our crew and tonight I had a scheduled class meeting. Sorry, Sir."

Skipper was great. He asked Neil to tell us about it since no one but his bunkmates knew anything about his algebra class, and he said, "It's no big deal. Some of our guys asked me if I would do it and I said 'sure.' No big deal."

On some of our first combat missions over North Korea out of Task Force 77, I enjoyed having Neil as my wingman. He was always there – dependable and alert. (Good aviator for a Midshipman.) I was not flying with him when he had his "adventure" but was airborne on another strike with my division, all of us being on the same tactical radio frequency. Neil and his foursome were strafing up some boxcars in the Wonsan freight yards when an ugly black ball of anti-aircraft fire over the nose of his plane distracted him for a second. That's all it took for Neil to push over slightly at 400 knots and 200 feet of altitude. He didn't even see the smoke stack that sheered about six feet off his port wing. Fortunately, he had enough aileron control to keep him out of the ground, and he climbed out of the area to the quasi-safety of the Wonsan harbor as his flying buddies gathered around his plane like mother hens.

Neil, with all the experience of a midshipman in combat, confronted two major problems: (1) He had live rockets aboard which he could not jettison; and (2) his stall speed, clean configuration, was above 200 knots.

It was quickly apparent that he could not land his plane either aboard ship or on a friendly runway south of the DMZ. He had one choice: Bail out.

Neil was escorted by his divisionmates along the coast of Korea southward to an allied airfield known as K-3. There, under conditions controlled as best they could be, Neil leveled off at 8,000 feet, 225 knots, heading past the outskirts of K-3, then ejected from his injured F9F-2 Panther. According to his flying mates, seat separation from the Panther was nominal and moments later Neil pushed himself away from his seat and pulled his ripcord. The 'chute opened beautifully.

As his buddies circled Armstrong in his descending parachute, they said something fell away from Neil. It turned out to be his helmet. As he explained to us later, he had learned from the parachute school that pilots often lost their helmets during ejection, but he still had his on. Wrong, he thought. So he took off his helmet and threw it down as he descended.

Neil landed softly in a moist rice paddy and was quickly picked up and returned to the K-3 air base, uninjured. Within hours, a South Korean peasant who had witnessed this event, saw Neil's helmet bounce nearby his hootch, picked it up and returned it to K-3 and finally to Neil.

The following day, Armstrong was flown out to the *Essex* in a TBM Cod, helmet and all, to a warm welcome from his squadronmates. All in the day of a Midshipman, he said. A day later, he was back on the flight schedule and teaching algebra at night in the crew quarters. A few weeks later, his commission came through and he became Ensign Neil Armstrong, USNR.

In the years which passed, Neil's life seemed to hang from parachutes. While in training for the Apollo mission, Neil was practicing in a lunar lander flying simulator in Houston, the "flying bedstead." when it went out of control at about 200 feet. Neil ejected safely from the thing just before it crashed, his 'chute deploying less than a hundred feet above the ground.

In the Gemini program, his Gemini 8 space vehicle went out of control with a stuck thruster while travelling almost 18,000 miles per hour. Neil regained control with some ingenious flying and made an emergency landing in the Pacific Ocean hundreds of miles from any recovery vessels; his spacecraft parachutes landing him gently in the Pacific swells.

In Apollo 11, after Neil became the first man to scuff up the moon, he and Buzz Aldrin and neat Mike Collins re-entered earth's atmosphere at some 25,000 miles an hour in their Apollo command module, which softly lowered its special cargo into the Pacific, supported by its three glorious parachutes.

From El Centro parachute school to the moon and back, lots of parachutes kept a very special man alive for us, and, for mankind.

One morning early in September, Major John Carpenter, our Air Force exchange pilot, Lieutenant (j.g.) Jim Ashford and I were launched from *Essex* on an armed reconnaissance mission from Tachon to Kangsong-ni, each of us carrying two 250-pound bombs plus a full load of ammo for our 20 mm guns located in the nose of the Panthers.

John Carpenter had flown 100 missions in F-80s and F-84s the previous year and was a fine Air Force representative to Naval carrier aviation and our squadron. Though he handled it admirably, he never got over the 150 foot catapult launches or landing in 300 feet on a pitching runway.

Jim Ashford was an eager young pilot with limited experience but with a strong desire to learn and to participate.

The plan was that as we let down over Tachon to initiate the reconnaissance run, Carpenter would go low, about 300 feet; I would be the middle man at 1,500 feet; and Ashford the tail-end Charlie at 2,500 feet. Should Major Carpenter spot a target such as tanks, trucks or commercial type buildings, he would call us and either Ashford or I would push over for the first run, bombing or strafing, with the other two planes circling to pursue the attack as appropriate.

As we proceeded outbound from Tachon, we encountered a lot of small arms fire, mostly machine guns with ominous tracers marking every fourth or fifth bullet. The axiom was that it is the bullets you don't see that knock you down. Soon I felt a mild clunk and saw that ground fire had punched holes in the top of my port tip tank – fortunately, the top of the tank. Ashford reported a hole in his starboard wing. It was apparent the guys on the ground had done this before.

About ten minutes into this recco run, Carpenter reported excitedly that there was a truck on the road ahead and asked if either Jim or I could get it. There was a steep hill to the left of the roadway, extending about 1,000 feet high and some quarter mile in width. I was not in position to make the run, but Ashford said he was. I flew to the left of the mini-mountain, joining Carpenter in circling for an attack on the truck, which we then could not see because of the terrain.

Ashford called, "Rolling in."

In moments, there was a terrific fireball, dark red and black, extending high into the air. I called, "Great work, Jim," but received no reply. As Carpenter and I came around the mini-mountain, we immediately saw why there was no response from Jim Ashford. There was the truck, still intact, and about 500 yards away was the fiery scattered wreckage of an F9F-2 Panther from VF-51. There was no parachute, no time for an ejection, not enough altitude for an ejection, no way Ashford could have survived. He had apparently caught machine gun fire in his run on the truck and simply dove into the ground at more than 300 knots at a 40-degree angle. Carpenter and I made a 360-degree turn to the right, dove on the truck and blew it to pieces with our 20 mm cannon. Carpenter destroyed it, and I destroyed the wreckage and the debris around it out of anger and frustration. I kept thinking, "What a price to pay for a goddam truck."

Back aboard *Essex*, Carpenter and I agreed – Jim Ashford was dead. We did not see his body in the carnage but we realized he had no chance of survival under the circumstances of the crash. We were asked more than once if Ashford should be classified as missing in action. Major Carpenter and I completely agreed that he would not have survived and that to declare Jim Ashford as MIA would be unjust, unfair and unrealistic. It would not be moral to give any lingering hope to his family that Jim might still be alive and might show up some years later. We would not subject them to that kind of suffering and hope in a hopeless cause.

After lunch that same day, three fine pilots took off from the *Essex* on a reconnaissance flight from a point southwest of Wonsan terminating in "Death Valley" to the south. Leading the trio was Lieutenant Dick Wenzell, who subsequently became a chief test pilot with North American Aviation. Number two man was Lieutenant (j.g.) Tom Hayward who was to become Chief of Naval Operations some years later, and number three was Lieutenant (j.g.) Ott Bramwell, smooth pilot, close friend of Hayward's throughout their four years together at the Naval Academy and their year of flight training.

The route they were to fly was "Red Two," which was patrolled several times a week by our armed reconnaissance Panthers because of its importance to the Communists. The plan was that Bramwell would start out as low man, Wenzell would be in the middle, and Tom Hayward high man, some 2,000 feet above and behind Bramwell.

The three had just entered "Red Two" and within minutes as Bramwell rolled left around a hill to follow the road below, the sky opened up with anti-aircraft fire. It was a flak trap.

Both Hayward and Wenzell saw Bramwell's Panther, flying at 300 knots and 500 feet, almost blown apart by anti-aircraft fire. They saw Ott's plane roll inverted, nose down into the ground. Just before the impact they saw the canopy come off indicating Bramwell had initiated the ejection process. He was inverted, no more than 100 feet above the terrain, more than 300 knots. Too late. The explosion was typical of that kind of crash – an ugly black and red fireball extending the length of the scattered debris. Hayward and Wenzell had their own problems trying to escape the heavy ground fire. Both their Panthers took many hits: Wenzell's fourteen and Hayward's nine, but they flew out of that valley of death.

Back aboard *Essex* there was disbelief in the readyroom. We had departed the States with twenty-four pilots, and in one day – one very bad day – less than three weeks into the war, we were down to twenty-two pilots. It was devastating. Tom Hayward had lost his closest friend, had watched him killed; our squadron had lost a fine young pilot; his wife and children had lost their loved one. We had lost Jim Ashford; his family had lost a son. And none of it made any sense to the twenty-two of us remaining. That day was a bad day.

The next morning six of us took off on a mission of revenge. We were armed as well as a Panther could be armed and we were going to destroy every gunner in that valley. We rolled into the corridor armed and ready. Just fire, you sons of bitches. Just shoot at us.

Not one shell came up from the ground. Not a single bullet. We circled the area, could see the wreckage of Ott's plane, but could find not one gun emplacement or a single living soul below. Stupid war.

A few days after we lost Bramwell and Ashford, the Korean War ended for me, at least for a couple of years. As told in Chapter One, on September 16, 1951, an F2H-1 Banshee leaped over the barrier on a bad landing and crashed into the Panther in which I was sitting; exploded, killed and injured too many pilots and flight deck crewmen. The Banshee pilot also died. Two months later, I was flown home to San Diego on a stretcher.

Before VF-51 returned to the States, two more of our fine young pilots would be shot down and killed. We had gone to the Korean fray in 1951 with twenty-four well-trained pilots and came home with nineteen. The other squadrons in our Air Group suffered comparable losses. It was not a good tour.

VIII

KOREA II

During training for a second tour with VF-51 in the Korean thing, we were flying Grumman F9F-5 Panthers out of NAS Miramar and NAS El Centro. Our new boss for this cruise was Commander George Duncan. A double ace in the Pacific during World War II, the Skipper was a force to be reckoned with and listened to.

Duncan had just completed a tour in the Bethesda Naval Hospital, having caught a rising ramp while landing an F9F-5 during flight tests aboard an *Essex*-class carrier out of Norfolk. His Panther had struck the ramp and broken in half, with only the cockpit rolling up the deck in a ball of fire with George still strapped aboard.

He was severely burned but undaunted. He'd brought his scarred-up body out to Air Group Five and was ready to go to war again. The Skipper and I had one thing in common – we were both fresh out of hospitals recovering from burns (Chapter One) – and that was about all we had in common since he was more experienced, more accomplished, and wiser about things that fly than this new Lieutenant.

Skipper introduced me to the Ground Control Approach, GCA, flown in formation. I had made GCAs before by myself but never with another plane on my wing.

The Ground Control Approach, in its day, was a remarkable medium for steering pilots to a safe landing in the face of inclement weather. Still is, but newer systems have supplemented or replaced this personalized landing approach tool. Yet for those of us who have lived or might have died during an approach in rotten weather, GCA may have been out-of-sight but not out of mind. Here is how my GCA with our Skipper occurred:

"Moore," Skipper sez, "I'm going on a cross-country to McCord Air Force Base in Tacoma, Washington, Saturday morning and I'd like you to come with me."

Commander Duncan's wish was my command. So off we went in two F9F-5s; the plan being that the Skipper would be the leader up to Tacoma and I would lead returning to Miramar. Nice trip and good weather to Tacoma Saturday morning, not good returning Sunday night on my watch.

Duncan was flying a loose wing as we cruised at 31,000 feet, flying south at 10:30 p.m. Sunday night. We could see the glow of Los Angeles on the cloud cover from 200 miles away. From over Los Angeles, we could see San Diego's glow as it brightened the 4,000-foot cloud layer covering the entire area, including the mountains to the east. The ceiling over our destination, NAS Miramar, was reported to us as being a comfortable 500 feet, which was GCA territory.

The commander moved in a little closer as the GCA controller picked us up, leveling us off at 6,000 feet on an easterly heading out of San Diego. It seemed to me we flew east at 250 knots an inordinate amount of time, perhaps as much as ten minutes, before the controller vectored us back westward for a final approach to Miramar's duty runway. The glow of San Diego's lights through the clouds seemed a long way off to me. Skipper, flying close formation, said nothing.

As soon as we were steady on a westward heading, the controller said, "You are on your final approach, commence your let-down at 500 feet per minute. Establish your landing configuration. Do not acknowledge further transmissions."

We started to let down, but I did not lower wheels and flaps because it just did not look right to me. Skipper was silent. When we got to the top of the cloud layer I leveled off. Duncan was still flying a close wing. I called the controller and advised him that we had leveled off because I thought we were too far east for a final approach, perhaps even over the mountains. (We were.)

The controller responded (this from the recording tapes), "Roger, turn right to three six zero for positive identification." We turned north. After about thirty seconds, the voice from the ground spoke, "Roger, Sugar One

Zero Five, we were tracking the wrong planes. Sorry. Turn left to one eight zero."

Skipper never said a word. We got properly and correctly oriented, made a successful approach and each landed safely. In the readyroom, I asked Duncan if he was aware that GCA was about to fly us into the mountains and he said, "Yup." I asked politely why he had not said a word if he knew.

"Johnny Boy," said he, "if you had gone into those clouds one inch I would have said plenty. I wasn't going to let you fly us into the mountains."

"But I still don't understand why you didn't tell me during our letdown."

"Because," he said, "I wanted to see how you were going to handle it."

George Duncan, Squadron Commander, leader extraordinaire.

Next day Duncan paid a visit to the Ground Control Approach unit; one they may still remember.

Fighter pilots who have spent many hours airborne alone or with a radar operator in the rear seat fly with considerable confidence in that mode, but put into the left seat of a small private plane with the wife in the right seat and the kids in the back seats, they become less confident, apprehensive and even uncomfortable, particularly when the weather is bad. The cargo then is a hell of a lot more substantive than a mere thirty million dollar fighter plane.

Some years later, during my test pilot days at North American, four of us test pilots owned a Cesna 310, a delightful, reliable machine with twice as many fans as our Bonanza had (which the 310 replaced), giving us twice as much comfort when we were roaring around with families aboard.

On one memorable flight I had in the 310, on board was my wife Marilynn and LaWanda Sievert. We were on our way from Columbus, Ohio, to Houston, Texas, where we would meet La's husband Morris. From Houston, it would be on to Acapulco for a week's vacation.

Less than an hour out of Houston, I was advised that a low overcast had moved in over the airport and the field had gone IFR – Instrument Flight Rules. But with a ceiling of 800 feet, I thought there should not be a problem. I'd just use GCA.

By the time we were overhead Houston, the ceiling had lowered to 200 feet with the cloud layer 4,000-feet thick. I had not made a GCA approach in several years and tried not to convey my uneasiness to my beautiful passengers. I was not comfortable. The task was not made any easier by my having to listen to the ground controller and my passengers all talking to me at the same time. The, "Where are we's?" and "How much furthers?" from within blended poorly with the, "Turn right two degrees," from without during final approach. With gear and flaps down in the landing configuration, I was balancing gyro horizon, gyro compass, rate-of-climb and air speed with, "It's hot in here," and "I can't see a thing."

I had to give the girls a task to occupy their minds so I told them to watch for the red approach light track, which led to the end of the runway, and tell me when they saw it. At an altitude of about 250 feet in the approach, just before I was going to be waved off, I heard two shrieks.

"There it is! There it is!"

Scared the wits out of me. Sure enough the runway loomed dead ahead and we landed safely. Then I had to listen for several days to how the girls had made the GCA approach and found the runway for me.

We were doing carrier qualification (car-quals) in the F9F-5s aboard the *Valley Forge* out of San Diego one foggy afternoon just weeks before we would depart for WestPac and Task Force 77 stationed off the east coast of North Korea.

I had completed my eight arrested landings and had stationed myself appropriately in vulture's row some five decks above the flight deck of the "Happy Valley" from whence to kibitz the struggles of my squadronmates in the landing pattern as they tried to qualify aboard.

It was not easy. Some of our younger pilots were having a difficult time in their Panthers trying to accommodate the heaving flight deck being given to us by the Pacific Ocean, the compelling signals from our LSO (Landing Signal Officer, alias "Paddles"), and the 400 foot landing area on the Valley, then a straight-deck carrier.

For this operation, there was established a "bingo" fuel, the minimum fuel load in the Panther which would allow a pilot to divert safely to NAS Miramar or North Island should he not be able to land on the carrier for any reason. And under these circumstances, a pilot diverted to the beach would have a squadronmate in another Panther accompany him so that he would not be alone should he encounter trouble enroute to a safe landing ashore.

Car quals did not always go smoothly, and some pilots could not handle the complexities of carrier landings, would not qualify, and would be left behind. On this early afternoon, one of our youngsters, Ensign Bill Blair, was having a tough time. And we were aware that weather conditions at the North Island and Miramar airfields were deteriorating but were still VFR, Visual Flight Rules, although marginal.

After six successive wave-offs because of erratic approaches, Bill reached his "bingo" fuel level and was directed to proceed to NAS Miramar. He would be accompanied by Dick Matthews, another bright young Ensign who had made four fine approaches in his Panther and was halfway to being qualified.

In the brief time it took the two planes to rendezvous, climb to 15,000 feet and set up cruise speed enroute to Miramar, the San Diego fog had rolled in and the air station went first to IFR (instrument rules), followed by the field being closed when ceiling and visibility went to zero - zero.

The two pilots were advised of the extreme weather conditions and directed to proceed to NAS El Centro in the desert about seventy miles east of Miramar.

Bill responded that he did not have enough fuel to reach El Centro and that he would make an instrument approach to Miramar. Matthews advised that he would proceed to El Centro and if he flamed out enroute, he would abandon his airplane and would keep ground control informed.

Ensign Bill Blair attempted three Ground Control Approaches to Miramar against the strong advice not to do so. He could be heard passing by the control tower in the dense fog, but he did not have a chance. After his third approach, he reported east of the airfield that he was ejecting from his Panther because it had flamed out from fuel starvation. Aboard ship, we were continuously updated about Bill's circumstance and were advised he had bailed out.

There was an agonizing hour's wait after Bill ejected, until word came that his body had been found close to a highway, still strapped to his ejection seat. Nothing automatic in those days. Following ejection, the pilot had to disconnect his seat belt, throw it and his shoulder harness aside, push away from the ejection seat, hope the radio wires and oxygen mask would separate, then pull the rip-cord to deploy his parachute. For Bill, there was not enough time or altitude. The Panther crashed into the hills east of Miramar and exploded. They always do.

Matthews, unaware of the happenings at Miramar, declared an emergency approach at NAS El Centro and made a safe landing there in the typical clear weather of that environment. His Panther flamed out as he turned off the runway.

Aboard the un-Happy Valley our CO, George Duncan, was coordinating the events to follow: recovery of the body, notification of next-of-kin, press releases, the kinds of things Skippers do. George had done it before. He was adamant that Blair's next-of-kin, his mom and dad, be notified immediately by telegram and was assured they would be informed within the next two hours.

A wonderfully compassionate man, Duncan then worked out his own plan for expressing his feelings in this matter of intense sorrow and grief. He knew he could not leave our squadron operations aboard the carrier in this critical period of training. He was needed there. Commander Duncan called me into his presence and said that as soon as the weather became operational he would have me catapulted in one of our Panthers for destination Miramar.

Skipper was loud and clear with his instructions. He wanted me to land at Miramar, wait until 9:00 p.m., then call Mr. and Mrs. Blair at their home in Los Altos, California. The telegram from the Navy's Chief of Naval Operations bearing the tragic news would have been in their hands for several hours, and I was to offer them the condolences of Commander Duncan and our squadron and the Navy. George emphasized that it was to be a very personal call on his behalf. I understood.

About 6:00 p.m., we received word that Miramar was open. I was catapulted in F9F-5 number S-106, no escort, and flew to Miramar where, with the help of the GCA troops guiding me through the clouds, I landed safely.

Shortly after 9:00 p.m., I dialed the Blair home. A man answered the telephone.

I asked, "Is this the Blair residence?"

The man said, "Billy, is that you?"

"Is this Mr. Blair?" I asked.

He responded that it was and apologized to me for thinking it might be his son calling. The telegram had not arrived.

I remember the conversation vividly.

"Mr. Blair, I am Lieutenant John Moore and I deeply regret having to tell you that your son was killed this afternoon in a plane crash. Our Skipper, Commander Duncan, asked that I call you to express his profound regrets."

Mr. Blair said, "Oh, no. Oh, no," and then was silent. He hung up the phone.

It was the worst and most painful telephone call I ever made.

On January 1, 1953, Our Air Group 5 aboard the *Valley Forge*, CVA 45 joined Task Force 77 off the east coast of Korea. Happy New Year, you Commie bastards – we're back! It would be our squadron's (VF-51) third combat cruise in the Korean thing, my second. Our F9F-5 Panthers would see their first combat and as it turned out, they would do well.

It was discouraging for us to find that nothing had changed in more than a year in the Korean War except that there was more anti-aircraft fire, the peace talks were rambling on, same DMZ, and more people being killed. Stupid war.

I had my own division of four planes and the pleasure of having Lieutenant (j.g.) Ernie Russell as my section leader. On one of our first strikes of this cruise, my division was assigned a target on the outskirts of a city named Hungnam. It was an ammo dump and was damn well defended. The commie gunners were waiting for us, but we managed to set off several explosions and start sixteen fires according to the records. But we really got shot up. As we left the target area, Ernie came alongside my plane – his Panther looked like a sieve and was streaming fuel from beneath the fuselage and both tip tanks.

I called "feet wet" to the Carrier and declared an emergency to get Ernie aboard the Happy Valley as quickly as possible. Ernie made it all the way to the downwind leg alongside the *Valley Forge*, had wheels down, flaps down, hook down, when he ran out of fuel and flamed out. I was right behind him and saw the huge splash as the Panther hit the water and flipped upside down. As I passed over, I saw Ernie pop to the surface. Whew! The helo picked him up and he was bruised but okay. For our valiant efforts I got a medal. Ernie got wet.

*　　　　*　　　　*

On a cold dismal morning in February '53, I led a formidable strike against a target just east of Wonsan on the coast of Korea. Our F9F-5 Panthers were each armed with two 250-pound general purpose bombs. We really weren't much compared to the AD Skyraiders, which could carry 8,000 pounds of bombs each. But it was only a war.

The gambit was, as usual, to attack from over land toward the water in the event anti-aircraft fire picked any of us off and we had to eject. Our plan: One run, drop both bombs, get the hell out of the area which always generated a lot of flak, some of it accurate and scary.

We reached a condition we called "feet dry" (over land) at 15,000 feet, which seemed to piss off the enemy anti-aircraft gunners who abandoned their chopsticks and Rice Krispies long enough to fill the air with bright tracers and black 37 mm puffs. I led this four-plane armada around into a fifty degree dive from a loose echelon, speed brakes out, stuff properly armed, and zeroed in on our target – an ammo dump. Lots of flak was annoying but I released my two powerful 250 pounders from about 3,000 feet and pulled hard on the stick to continue living.

While still flying in the gray-out regime during pull-up, I heard my number four man behind me radio that I had missed Korea. I pulled into a steep right bank and looked below for my bomb hits. A few hundred feet off shore two sizeable holes in the water were easily visible.

Another voice came over the radio. A voice I recognized. It was one of my roommates who was flying combat air patrol over the task force and was monitoring our frequency as well as CAPs. To my dismay I heard my roomie relay that info to the carrier, "Crabapple Base."

By the time we got back to the carrier, it seemed the entire fleet knew of my dive-bombing prowess. I came aboard and as I folded the Panther's wings and taxied forward, some yellow-shirt deckhand held up a sign that read, "You missed the whole goddam country?"

I took more flak in the readyroom debriefing than I did over the target. But even in war, sometimes you gotta laugh. As the dust settled and the razzing stopped, it was back to business as usual in the air war over Korea.

I had no idea how our intelligence officer, a bright lieutenant (j.g.) named Ken Brownell, would report my fiasco and did not ask. Some weeks later, however, my wife mailed me a newspaper clipping from a local paper in San Diego, which I still have. It reported in part that Lieutenant John Moore had led a strike of four jets against part of the enemy's food chain, a fish hatchery near Wonsan, and scored direct hits with his bombs which caused significant damage to the Communist aggressors. No medals were awarded.

VF-51 had some extraordinary commanding officers in its sixty-two year history. I was privileged to serve with two of them: Lieutenant Commander Ernie Beauchamp during my first Korean tour in 1951; then Commander George Duncan in 1953 as we returned to the Korean fray aboard the *Valley Forge*. Both of these skippers were disciplinarians, yet personable, and both had a great sense of humor. Thank God.

After our first thirty-day tour on the line with Task Force 77 operating off the east coast of North Korea, the Happy Valley returned to the Navy base in Yokosuka, Japan, for a week of R and R (Rest and Rehabilitation). On the second night of liberty in the city of Yokosuka, Skipper ordered all our pilots not on duty to report to a popular geisha house in the center of town for sushi and "hota sake."

"We're going to have a squadron meeting," he said.

It was, "Aye, aye, Captain, see you there."

Some of us arrived early and were sitting around on the floor mats sipping sake when one of the girls asked about our Skipper and wanted to know when he would be there and what we called him. An ensign piped up, "Well, he's a knucklehead so we call him 'knucklehead.'" All laughed and giggled because we knew George Duncan was anything but a knucklehead. But the very pretty geisha girl, beautifully attired, giggled delightfully and said, "Ah, so, we will call him 'Knucksan.'"

Soon "Knucksan" arrived with our exec and was greeted by the lovely girl with, "Ah so, Knucksan, welcome."

In the course of the evening, Skipper was Knucksan to the refreshing young girls but "Sir" or "Skipper" to us pilots. George asked what it meant and was advised by the geisha girls that it was a term of endearment. George was skeptical.

Throughout the rest of the six-month tour, he was Knucksan behind his back – but never to his face.

Knucksan had some very strong opinions about how his squadron would fight the war. His clearly stated objectives were to do as much damage as possible to the enemy but bring all our pilots back safely. Period. That meant one bombing run – whether with two, four or six bombs, no matter. Drop them all in one run ON the target and get out – from now on. Not six bombs, six runs. Stupid, Knucksan sez. "Just do it right the first time and get out."

It was truly ironic and tragic that we lost one pilot on this cruise – a talented young lieutenant (j.g.) named Ken Gedney, who was number four man in Duncan's division. In a well-coordinated attack on an industrial target in "Death Valley" south of Wonsan (when Knucksan led an attack you can bet it was well-coordinated), the first three pilots pulled out through some intense ground fire. Ken did not. He was hit and went straight in. We knew that Duncan was devastated but he did his best not to show it.

On the final day of our six-month cruise with Task Force 77, after all planes were safely aboard, we got a written direction from our commanding officer to report to the readyroom at 1700 hours for a squadron meeting. It was an order – delivered to each pilot personally. It was signed "Knucksan."

We immediately contacted our executive officer to find out what kind of trouble we might be in, and how Commander Duncan knew about Knucksan. Said our Exec, "He's known about it all along. He loves it."

Knucksan, you were something else.

By early spring of 1952, I had become an outpatient from the Balboa Naval Hospital in San Diego and had been designated our squadron's (VF-51) representative ashore in the U.S. and A. while my squadronmates continued the war with Task Force 77 off North Korea. When the squadron returned to San Diego, it would be assigned to the new master jet site then under construction at NAS Miramar, along with the other squadrons of Air Group Five. We would transition to the newer model of the Panther, the F9F-5, and prepare to return to the Korean fray.

In charge of the construction of the first master jet site was Lieutenant Commander John G. Dillon, United States Navy, Civil Engineer Corps. Jack Dillon was one bright guy and for a civil engineer, easy for a lowly Naval Lieutenant aviator to communicate with. For reasons totally unfathomable to me, we became great friends as "we" made NAS Miramar operational; he a construction type and me a burned-up Navy pilot fresh out of the hospital.

Since I was at that time one of the few Air Group Five officers around for purposes of coordination, I spent considerable time in Jack's office trying to explain that he was building Miramar for airplanes, not for Pentagon left-overs seeking asylum in San Diego. I did learn quickly that he was very aware of that fact and, indeed, he bent backward over a lot of blueprints to accommodate his Navy's fly-boys.

For example, one day I explained to the "Commander" that each squadron would need a line shack, a facility for our line crewmen where they could store their tie-down lines, chocks, rags, engine duct and tail covers, and have a place to rest their asses and drink coffee between flights during day and night operations. Jack got out the blueprints for line shacks, which defined buildings better than the home I shared with my family. He said, "You want that tomorrow?" I said hell no, and Jack asked me to tell him what we could get by with. I defined storage bins, benches, coffee pots, telephone stuff – bare minimums.

The next morning a trail of four tractors kicking up dust that could be seen in LaJolla came around one of the hangars, each tractor towing a sizeable building on skids – one for each squadron – each equipped with the storage bins I'd asked for – in fact, everything I had requested. He had converted four of his storage buildings overnight into line shacks. From his jeep all Dillon said was, "Where do you want them?"

Jack had a way of expressing impatience. I would call him from our hangar with a problem, and he would say, "Okay, get over here right away and we'll discuss it." I never could get over to his excellency's presence soon enough, so I learned to drive over to his office, then call him from his secretary's phone. When he ordered me into his presence, I simply walked into his office – a distance of fifteen feet. He didn't think it was funny.

The Dillon and Moore families ended up socializing, and we developed a wonderful and unusual friendship which has survived more than fifty years. At first it seemed Dillon and I had little in common; he a builder of air stations and I just an airplane driver, but it became a bonding based on mutual respect, I think.

For example, after our squadron reformed at Miramar in early 1952, we found the 8,000 foot runways sometimes too short for our younger pilots, and we lost a couple of Panthers as they ran off the end of the runway into the soft sand shearing the landing gear. One Friday afternoon, I invited the commander to take a jeep ride with me out to the end of the east-west runway where a number of skid marks were clearly visible, made by pilots locking brakes while trying to get stopped before running into the sand. I asked him if there were any possibility of extending the runway maybe three hundred feet, which would have saved six or seven airplanes and doubtlessly would save others. There is something meaningful and ominous about skid marks.

The following Monday morning, a contractor team was levelling the over-run on that runway, and by Wednesday afternoon we had a 400 foot asphalt over-run in place. Some months later, I took Jack out there again in his jeep to see the skid marks which extended into the asphalt. No damage done. Good move, Dillon.

In this period, Jack and I experimented with gin drinks in a blender, adding bananas, strawberries and orange juice for flavor, until finally concocting the perfect drink by adding cranberries to the mixture. We agreed. The cranberries did it. No question.

When the *Valley Forge* carrying Air Group Five returned to San Diego from my second Korean tour in the summer of 1953 to be greeted by several thousand cheering wives, mothers, fathers, children, et al., there was no problem finding my brood on the dock. They were holding up a five-by-fifteen foot sign with Cranberries written on it; one end held by Jack and Fran Dillon, the other by my clan. Welcome home, John.

In years to come, we stayed in touch, yet rarely got our families together. In the Vietnam War, Rear Admiral Jack Dillon was head man for the Navy civil engineers in Nam, building roads, ammo dumps and the like for our forces in that ugly war. My son Randy was an Army Sergeant in the jungle somewhere near the DMZ whilst the Admiral was leading his gang of construction types putting together roads through the muck of South Vietnam. Just before Jack was to complete his tour of command and be assigned to the wars of the Pentagon, he determined where Randy's infantry platoon was located in the jungle, climbed into his helicopter accompanied by two helo gunships, and set out to find Randy. He flew over angry territory to find my son, who had been advised that an "0-8"(two-star Admiral or General) was enroute to see him. Randy said, "I don't even know an 0-8!"

Admiral Dillon's helicopters set down a few hundred yards from Randy's position. The two met and spoke together for all of five minutes. Then the Admiral was airborne again. He returned to his base safely with only nine bullet holes in his helicopter. By God, I don't think I would have done it. Thank you, Jackson.

The Admiral left the Navy with great dignity, only the second officer in the history if the Navy Civil Engineer Corps to be awarded two Distinguished Service Medals. I sent him a bushel of cranberries.

Commander George Duncan, Knucksan, was more than supportive and kind to me. He recommended to the Navy's Bureau of Personnel and to the Navy Test Pilot School Administration that I be accepted as a student in Class 11 of the School at the Naval Air Test Center, Patuxent River, Maryland. And so, once home with my family in San Diego, we packed our worldly goods and departed for Pax River and the Test Pilot School. Thank God Korea was behind me. Not so for the 54,000 Americans killed there, the 100,000 wounded, or the more than 8,000 still listed as Missing in Action. Stupid war. And we didn't even win it. We, as a nation, would never again get involved in a war like Korea. Would we?

IX

PAX RIV

The Naval Air Test Center at NAS Patuxent River, Maryland, was and still is the primary flight testing facility for Naval aviation. The purpose of the Test Center, referred to as NATC or Pax Riv, is to determine serviceability of new Navy airplanes for use in the fleet prior to their being released to fleet squadrons.

I was assigned to the Test Pilot School's Class 11 in 1953, along with twenty-five other Navy, Marine, and civilian pilots scheduled for six months of intense ground school and flight training oriented toward making us test pilots. Inasmuch as only about fifty pilots a year were accepted as students by the Navy Test Pilot School's directors, it was considered an honor and a privilege to be included in this small, select student body. In fact, all of the Mercury, Gemini, and Apollo astronauts were graduates of either the Navy or the Air Force Test Pilot Schools.

In 1953, there were four principal Test Divisions at Pax Riv: Flight, Service, Armament, and Electronics. All were staffed by pilots who had graduated from the Test Pilot School. It is important to mention that there was a third test pilot school in the world with a quality comparable to the Navy and Air Force Schools. It was the British Test Pilot School of England, which was a class act then and I understand still is.

My luck held out, for I was assigned to the Carrier Suitability Branch of the Flight Test Division upon graduation. During the following two years, I flew some fascinating test programs for the Navy.

In early 1954, Lieutenant Tom Hayward, Bob Rostine's and my squadronmate and roommate on the carriers *Essex* and *Valley Forge* during

141

the Korean event, joined us at the Naval Air Test Center. Rostine was flying the carrier suitability trials on the F7U-3 Cutlass; I had just graduated with Class ll from the Test Pilot School and was headed for the Flexdeck Program; and Hayward ended up the main man in Class l2 before going on to the Flying Qualities Branch of the Flight Test Division at the Test Center.

Haywood evading Flexdeck, spent the next two years boring holes through the clouds with a number of exotic flying machines (such as the Douglas XF5D), most of which none of us lesser beings ever saw. Rostine also avoided the bouncy program, and flew the Cutlass carrier trials (as Charles Lindbergh might have) before becoming a civilian test pilot. I was assigned to make wheels-up landings onto a rubber deck, a program totally unfathomable to an average "hooker" like myself. (Quality won out in the end: Tom Hayward eventually became Chief of Naval Operations, Rostine became chief test pilot for Chance Vought, and on down the line I became the Mayor of Cocoa Beach, Florida.)

The Navy Flexdeck Program was only flown by three pilots – John Norris, a civilian test pilot from Grumman whose accounts of his flying activities are totally unreliable; a Marine type named Bob Feliton who had a proclivity for wheels-up landings anyway; and the author of this treatise who will make every effort to play down his heroics in this, the lost chord of Naval aviation's wonderfully orchestrated history.

I ended up with the dubious distinction of having made more wheels-up landings in land-based jet airplanes than any other American. Although my wheels-up landings were deliberate and carefully monitored by the Navy, I am not inclined to brag about the achievement to aviators for obvious reasons – they think I am loony!

It seemed that in the early post World War II era, paralleling the development of a reliable afterburning device to improve fighter aircraft performance, an enlightened group of scientists, obviously not aeronauts, concluded that the most inefficient, least productive part of a fighter plane was the landing gear system. A marked improvement in a fighter plane's performance, they concluded, could be easily obtained if a fighter could be designed with no landing gear – no brakes, no oleos, no wheels, no hydraulics, no beefy airframe structure. After all, what purpose did this useless excess weight serve during an intercept mission at high altitude? Empirical data indicated that the performance of a sweptwing jet fighter such as the

Grumman F9F-8 might be improved by as much as fifty percent if this airplane had been designed without landing gear. This was an inspiring hypothesis!

An aggressive program was established involving the Navy, Air Force, and the British Naval Air Arm to study the feasibility of such a revolutionary concept and to look at the minor details such as how to take off and land this miracle weapon and what to do about ground handling procedures. Thus evolved a Zero Launch Program undertaken by the U.S. Air Force, which drew the short straw, and a Wheels-Up Landing Development Program, or perhaps better defined as a No-Wheels Landing Development Program, undertaken simultaneously by the Royal Aircraft Establishment, U.S. Navy and U.S. Air Force, with the British leading the way, as they often did in those days of 1953, '54 and '55.

Two Grumman F9F-7 sweptwing Cougars were assigned to the Navy program. They were standard production models modified by Grumman for the Flexdeck landings. The airplanes originally had Allison J-33 engines installed but were modified to accommodate the Pratt and Whitney J-48 jet engine because of: (1) Improved engine acceleration qualities in the J-48; and (2) the pilots' expressed desires for continuous engine operation during periods of flight. A number of other modifications were made to these machines such as adding a false flat bottom to the fuselage and modifications to the flap kinematics. As a surfer, it occurred to me more than once that if the engine flamed out during these operations, I might catch a wave with the flat bottom and curl up onto the beach.

At the Test Center at Patuxent, the Navy Flexdeck was constructed alongside the approach end of Runway No. 13. It was 570 feet long and eighty feet wide, made of thirty inch diameter pneumatic tubes that were inflated by all the air compressors in the state of Maryland. A single arresting cable was strung across the approach of the deck at a height of twelve to eighteen inches. Of particular interest to this pilot was the pneumatic approach ramp, a sort of round down with a gentle slope up to the deck and arresting cable.

I was told the purpose of this ramp was to accommodate a premature sinking touchdown by the airplane in the ramp area. In this event, the ramp's resilience would then allow the test vehicle to bounce high enough above the deck where an explosion of the Cougar would cause minimum damage to the deck although maximum damage to the pilot's ass was probable. On the other hand, a low, flat approach which resulted in airplane/ramp con tact produced the likelihood of the arresting cable, located immediately forward of the ramp, passing over the nose of the airplane and into the cockpit. This would result in the arresting loads being sustained primarily by the pilot's teeth. In flying the deck, thoughts of these prospects in the final approach tended to concentrate the mind.

As a young Navy Lieutenant my qualifications for flying the Flexdeck centered around having made several hundred carrier landings in various prop and jet aircraft, all on straight deck aircraft carriers. In these landings, my objective was to put the airplane anywhere aft on the carrier deck 'midst the arresting cables so that the airplane could be taxied, towed, or hoisted out of the landing area. For the Flexdeck Program, these goals were narrowed somewhat.

The arrested landing requirements for the Flexdeck with the Cougar were that the airspeed be controlled at 135 knots (plus or minus two knots) and the height over the deck, hook down, wheels up, was to be four feet (plus or minus six inches), with the airplane to be landed wings level on the thirty inch wide centerline stripe. Since this was a bit more constraining than just hitting an aircraft carrier, I made every effort to avail myself of information related to the progress of the on-going Zero Launch and Arrested Landing Programs being conducted by the Air Force in order to benefit from whatever experience they had which might be germane to the Navy program. It seemed safe to say the knowledge I gained by their efforts was somewhat less than confidence-building.

I was privileged to be an observer at Edwards Air Force Base for Phase II of the Air Force Zero Launch Program. Phase I had been somewhat successfully completed by the United States Air Force using a straightwing F-84 jet fighter as the missile. For Phase II, the Air Force chose the F-100 Super Sabre jet, and with wisdom commensurate with the maturity of this elite branch of the service, they selected a civilian test pilot to fly the test program – a prematurely gray-haired fellow named Al Blackburn of North American Aviation.

For this venture, the F-100 was perched on a launching pad, angled about 30 degrees skyward, and a solid-state rocket booster was strapped to the aft ventral side of the airplane immediately below the horizontal stabilizers. After Blackburn had been pushed into the cockpit and strapped in, the F-100 jet engine was started in preparation for launch. Blast-off was made with wheels down, which indicated to me some apprehension about the suc

The Grumman F11F-1 Tigercat, with John Moore aboard, is manhandled into position over the catapult of *Intrepid* for carrier trials.

ate 1956 at Columbus, Ohio, six North American test pilots pose: (l. to r.) Bill Ingram, Dick Venzell, Bill Morse, John Moore, George Hoskins, and Ed Gillespie. Only Moore and Gillespie urvived the dangerous occupation.

A North American FJ-4 Fury flamed out on take-off and John Moore (near the nose, reaching for his helmet) couldn't get it stopped before going off the runway.

In 1957, John Moore pilots an FJ-4F Fury with rocket engine on a test flight.

John Moore arrives in Palmdale, CA, for structural testing of the North American T2J-1 Buckeye.

The Buckeye in flight, author in the cockpit.

A closeup of experimental test pilot, John Moore in the North American RA-5C Vigilante.

The Vigilante, piloted by Ed Gillespie, rolls away from the camera of John Moore.

John Moore on the boarding ladder of a RA-5C in 1961. The rear canopy has been removed for ejection tests.

In a 1962 photo taken by the author, the fuel probe of his Vigilante can be seen as he approaches the drogue of an aerial tanker, another Vigilante.

Key members of the NASA/NAA launch team at Downey, CA in 1963 in the Apollo mock-up room. They are (l. to r.) Donnelly, Preston, Pyle, author Moore, Wiley and Dutton.

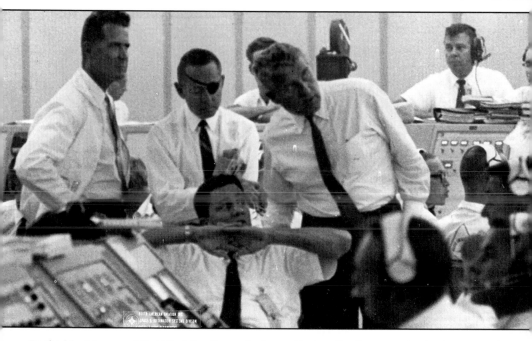

In the blockhouse of Pad 34 at the Kennedy Space Center, the foursome in the foreground are: (l. to r.) author Moore, Dale Meyers, NAA, Dr. Werner Von Braun (famed German rocket scientist) then with NASA, and (sitting) Merritt Preston of NASA.

Marilynn Moore

The author, 1967.

cess of the mission. Following afterburner ignition in the F-100, the solid booster was ignited initiating lift-off.

The first zero launch in the F-100 was a success in all respects with the spent booster being jettisoned at approximately 200 knots. A normal landing was made at Edwards after this marvelous achievement. Several other successful launches followed.

The final launch was also a gratifying success with one minor exception, i.e., failure of the booster rocket to jettison, which resulted in an aircraft center of gravity somewhere in the vicinity of the horizontal stabilizers. By the conclusion of this flight, Mr. Blackburn had demonstrated not only the zero launch capability of the F-100 but its ejection system as well, with both vehicle and pilot landing in the desert, although several miles apart. Blackburn ended up with bad ankles from the event, and the F-100 ended up with bad everything. This terminated the Zero Launch Program.

Having ingested all the glory of the Zero Launch Program I could assimilate, I was dispatched to the site of the Air Force Flexdeck Landing Program to observe these exciting undertakings and to hopefully benefit from their experience in such drama.

The Air Force was making final preparations for arrested landings into their inflated Flexdeck reluctantly provided by the Goodyear Tire and Rubber Company. They had selected the straightwing F-84G as their test vehicle, most likely because in the event of any loss, they had little to lose.

There was concern that damage would occur to the test vehicle's flaps following hook engagement with the arresting cable and subsequent deck/vehicle contact. Consequently, a microswitch was installed in the arresting hook face that would initiate flap retraction upon hook contact with the arresting cable, thus avoiding flap damage during landing. The result was that in the first attempted arrested wheels-up landing into the Goodyear deck, the hook struck the approach ramp, bounded over the arresting cable and returned to deck contact as the airplane flew by. The hook then encountered a puddle of water that had been sprayed on the deck for lubrication, the impact of which closed the microswitch in the hook and the flaps were retracted. The F-84 settled on the deck, dropped into the desert and ground to a halt in a large cloud of dust. The result was excessive damage to both pilot and test vehicle, putting both out of the program.

A second test vehicle was prepared and a second pilot willing to fly this mission was located, heroically armed with little knowledge of what had transpired to this point. Following a brief training program for the new pilot, the Air Force scheduled its second landing attempt.

In this landing, the hook successfully engaged the arresting cable, causing the F-84 to pitch violently into the deck on its nose for a series of three or four bounces before coming to a halt. Motion pictures showed that at first impact, the pilot, a tall lad who was strapped in snugly, disappeared completely in the cockpit. This left impressions of the pilot's lateral incisors in the top of the control stick and caused structural damage to his vertebrae. The result caused the hierarchy of a tailhookless Air Force to reconsider what the hell they were doing in this program anyway; wherewith they abandoned the whole thing, leaving further evaluation of this extraordinary concept in the capable hands of the United States Navy.

It should be stated that after observing these historic events of zero launch and wheels-up landings, this pilot did some soul searching for a reason as to why he should risk his cute little ass furthering this wacky program – and the answer was clear – stupidity.

An excellent introduction to the Flexdeck landing concept was offered by the British to the pilots who would fly the Navy program at Pax River. By the time our program had reached the hardware state, the British had made several hundred wheels-up landings into their deck at Farnborough, many of which were successful. Their test vehicle was the jet powered Vampire, a delightful little aeronautical innovation the English had hurriedly constructed in World War II to chase down buzz bombs being launched by the Germans toward the United Kingdom. It was like a toy. You felt like you were flying a jet made by Radio Shack.

I was assigned to a three-week stint in England to fly the British deck and was chaperoned by the late Marsh Beebe who was Director of Flight Test at the Naval Air Test Center at that time. It was a bit like being chaperoned by Errol Flynn. Marsh had been Commander of Air Group Five on the aircraft carrier *Essex* during one of my VF-51 tours in the Korean War, and I had flown wing on him several times as we strafed high-priority haystacks and burned-out railroad cars south of Wonsan. Marsh was among the best of the best.

Our initial flights in the Vampire were made at Boscomb Down under the tutelage of a "batsman," the equivalent of our Landing Signal Officer (LSO), who stood at the edge of the runway with two "bats" (and a fire extinguisher) as we made practice runs, wheels-up, in the little toy airplanes.

The best indication of being too low in a pass over the runway was the batsman's motion to arm the fire extinguisher, easily discernible with one's peripheral vision in the fly-by.

Following several days of practice at Boscomb Down, I ferried the Vampire to Farnborough as Marsh climbed into a sizable black automobile with darkened windows, piloted by a lady military type, and off they went in the direction of Farnborough. As it turned out, Farnborough was only about twenty minutes by Vampire and forty-eight hours by car.

Beebe and I were impressed by the courtesies extended to us by the British. At night, for example, before we retired in their Boscomb Down Officers' Quarters, we put our shoes outside the door and a gentleman called a batman came quietly by in the dark of night, picked them up, shined them gloriously, and had them ready for us in the morning as he came in to rouse us with a pot of tea. The similarity of names batsman and batman led Beebe to conclude we might broaden the responsibilities of our own batsmen (LSOs) at Pax River to include shoe shining, but the plan ran into some resistance from the likes of Bill Tobin, Sam Thompson and "Weakeyes" Boutwell, our own single-purpose Landing Signal Officers.

Related to the above, it is worth noting that shortly after returning from England, I was housed in the BOQ at Pax River for a few nights and I wondered what would happen there if I put my shoes outside the door as at Boscomb Down. And so I did. The next morning they were gone.

The English deck was configured quite differently from our own. It was higher in the middle than at each end, giving the pilot the impression he was landing on the hump of a bridge. The reason, of course, was that following arrestment, the deck in effect came up to meet the airplane, reducing the landing loads considerably.

The flight procedures at Farnborough were straightforward. One dry run was made over the Flexdeck with the wheels and arresting hook up at an approach speed of about 90 knots. On the next pass, the hook was lowered and in a straightaway of about 3,000 feet a ten degree glide slope was established with the airplane aimed at the center of the deck. Engagement was evident by the pitching down and rapid deceleration of the airplane followed by mild impacts and about a dozen bounces until the airplane halted, all in some 100 feet. It was a little like being dribbled by Magic Johnson.

The engine was then shut down and a cable was hooked to the nose of the Vampire allowing it to be winched off the deck onto a flatbed truck, the pilot remaining in the cockpit. The Vampire was then transported to some facility on the outskirts of the airport next to The Doxy Pub where a crane was off-loading sewer pipe from railway cars. The crane operator was gracious enough to pause the sewer operation and lift the Vampire from the truck. While suspended from the crane, I lowered the wheels and the airplane was lowered to the ground. The toy's engine was started, and the airplane taxied along the left side of the road (of course) back to the airport for another take-off and landing. Oncoming autos paid little heed to this ritual, simply pulling off onto the grass to clear the Vampire's wing. Marsh made six landings in this manner and I made eight, followed by an approved touch-and-go (bounce-and-go) landing, which I made to become familiar with that phenomenon, hopefully, never having to experience it on our own deck at Pax River.

The exercise proved quite beneficial as a training method in preparation for the American Navy program, although as it was to be subsequently determined, the speeds, energies, and kinematics involved with the F9F-7 and our deck were markedly different from those encountered at Farnborough.

Marsh Beebe did not fly the Navy deck at Pax River for reasons privy only to commanding officers but in all likelihood, because he found more important things to do. Smart man. Right stuff!

The first ten wheels-up landings into the Navy deck at Pax River were made by John Norris, Grumman test pilot and boy wonder, whose background was Navy aircraft carrier type with sound experience in arresting wires, barrier cables, and bent props on several aircraft carriers. John also availed himself of training on the British deck with the Vampire before beginning the tests in the F9F-7 Cougar at Pax River.

Prior to any landings in the Cougar, however, considerable thought was given to the results of the Air Force landings and the severe neck injuries their pilot had sustained as the airplane impacted the deck following arrestment. Analysis of this circumstance led us to believe our landings might well produce the same unsavory results. As a consequence, a sturdy aluminum device was fabricated to be worn by the pilot, designed as a back and head brace to protect his spine and neck from the kinds of injuries sustained in the Air Force landings. The protective metal harness extended from the cleavage in the pilot's buttocks to the top of his head.

A special helmet was also fabricated with a male probe in the back of the helmet, which was inserted by feel into a female receptacle in the protective brace, which allowed the pilot to lock his head to the back brace prior to an arrested landing. Both the back brace and helmet were molded to fit John Norris, but since he and I were about the same size, the special equipment also fit me fairly well except for the helmet, which seemed to be slightly square.

The operational procedure for using this equipment differed somewhat between Norris and myself. Norris would lock his head up on the downwind leg, then call in "turning base, wheels-up, head up and locked". I found that flying the base leg with my head locked in a fixed position was a little disorienting. It was as if the airplane were fixed in space and the horizon rotating around it. So I just flew a longer straightaway and locked my head up in the final approach. John Norris did not seem to find the approach as he flew it to be particularly disorienting, though in those memorable instances when I flew with John in other flying machines, he seemed to be disoriented a goodly part of the time anyway, so this seemed rather normal to him.

There was an anomaly associated with the protective harness related to its weight. It was calculated that with the harness on and the life jacket inflated (in the event of a water landing), the buoyancy was slightly negative. A simple procedure was developed to resolve this: Namely, in the event of a ditching and following the pilot's safe egress from the airplane, he had but to remove the life jacket, remove the parachute, remove the protective harness, reinstall the life jacket and inflate it. It was expected that this could be accomplished while the pilot was standing on the bottom of Chesapeake Bay.

Familiarization flights prior to arrested landings onto the rubber deck included making low passes over the regular runways at the Test Center with the wheels down at first, followed by wheels-up passes under the watchful eyes of our own "batsman," our Landing Signal Officer. These creatures could not contribute much to my wheels-up fly-bys which were made but three feet above the runway, because a high or low signal that related to a six-inch change in height above the deck was essentially meaningless to me. Considering the Cougar's close proximity to the ground in these passes, I was particularly disinterested in any flag waving by one of our LSOs, "Weakeyes" Boutwell. Bill Tobin was bad enough.

When the confidence level was as high as it was going to get, I commenced making wheels-up, hook-up passes over the Flexdeck, concentrating on being at the correct height, on centerline, at 135 knots, wings level, again under the watchful eyes of our LSOs. They had resorted to shouting instructions on the radio because of my inability to respond to their frantic flag waving. The concentration required on line up, height control, et al., was too demanding to permit me to shift my vision to the LSO for signals, and regardless of all the semaphore he generated, it could not be recorded by my peripheral vision or saturated mind. The radio communications were helpful to tell me what I had done but of little help in telling me what to do.

Airplane height control across the deck was not too difficult in smooth air but, as expected, became increasingly difficult as turbulence increased. Crosswinds helped very little as well. In moderate turbulence, I was unable to control the height over the deck any closer than about plus or minus a foot, and as a consequence, we made no arrested landings onto the deck except under very stringent atmospheric conditions related to wind direction and turbulence. Remembering normal flying conditions in the Sea of Japan or in the Atlantic off Bermuda where the carrier deck is never still, this program seemed more ludicrous with each passing day.

It was interesting that in the final approach during which exacting speed control of 135 knots was required along with other constants previously mentioned, the airspeed indicator seemed to be inaccessible. As best I could tell, it took about one and a half seconds to shift my focus of vision from outside flight parameters into the cockpit to locate, read and mentally record my airspeed, then shift my vision back to deck line-up and other constantly changing variables. At 135 knots that amounted to more than 300 feet of travel, and as every "hooker" (tailhook pilot) knows, a lot can happen in 300 feet when you are close to the carrier deck.

In an attempt to improve this condition, we mounted a very large airspeed indicator on the instrument panel hood, almost directly in the pilot's line of sight during final approach. It was hoped I could read this monster with peripheral vision but I could not. It did, however, reduce the time spent with eyes in the cockpit by a fraction of a second and that was helpful.

Although a level final approach was required to minimize the possibility of an inadvertent touch down, it was determined that a flat approach – two degrees or less – resulted in an inadequate view of the deck. Consequently, my final approach was extended to about two miles from the deck at an altitude of 1,000 feet, which gave me time to get my head up and locked and provided an adequate view of the deck for alignment and speed control. The Cougar leveled off about 2,000 feet from the approach ramp at 135 knots in a flight path parallel to the deck to prevent inadvertent contact with the deck before reaching the arresting cable. Analysis had indicated that a touchdown into the deck without an arrestment would result in the Cougar being unable to become airborne again because of the pilot's inability to attain sufficient angle of attack for flight. It was projected that this would put the Cougar into the sand trap adjoining the fifteenth green at the Pax River golf course where I had been many times before but never in a Cougar.

During my initial wheels-up arrested landings, I was not aware of wire engagement and not certain of arrestment until the Cougar had traversed approximately 120 feet of the landing mat. Then as the airplane was decelerated by the constant runout arresting gear, a pronounced nose down pitch into the deck occurred. Following deck contact, I was extraordinarily aware of the longitudinal pitching into and out of the deck. In the first few landings, statistical analysis indicated that the severity of impact could be directly correlated with the size of the wet spot which appeared on the front of the pilot's flight suit. The lack of pilot sensitivity to the decelerating forces was attributable to the protective harness and head lock.

A unique aspect from this pilot's standpoint was the impression, as the Cougar pitched into and out of the deck during arrestment, that the airplane was motionless and that it was the horizon which was in motion moving up and down past the airplane's nose.

The most severe landing in the Navy program occurred on the twentieth landing. For this test, I was to engage the wire at the maximum height possible, about five feet above the deck with the Cougar at its maximum design gross weight for these tests as adjusted by fuel loading. On this landing, I let the right wing drop slightly after hook engagement so that deck contact was made with a bank angle of about five degrees right wing down. Vehicle penetration on contact was twenty-five inches into the deck, five inches from bottoming out.

Pitching out of the deck the first time was accompanied by a pronounced left roll followed by a roll to the right on the second pitch out as a result of the left wing/deck contact. The rolling and pitching continued until the Cougar came to a halt, which seemed like about four days. It was a wild ride. Black rubber deck marks were found on the upper surface of the right wing. If the Air Force Flexdeck landings did not disprove the concept, this landing certainly did.

Finally, I made the twenty-third and last wheels-up landing onto the deck at Pax River in this noble enterprise, thus releasing all the firetrucks and meatwagons to their normal duties at the Air Station.

From the flying standpoint, there was impracticality to the concept almost from the beginning. Pilot skills demanded for successful landings on a stationary deck were stretched close to practical limits and, although the British had landed the Vampire on a Flexdeck at sea under calm conditions, the possibilities of successfully deploying a squadron of higher performance sweptwing jets on a Flexdeck aircraft carrier by our Navy had to be considered unfeasible.

Since I was the only Navy pilot to fly the Navy Flexdeck (John Norris - civilian), I made that statement without fear of contradiction. Yet as any carrier pilot would surmise, it was fun to fly.

In our Carrier Suitabililty Branch of Flight Test, the pilot's responsibilities included all facets of flight operations in determining whether a new model airplane was suitable for fleet service, including the minimum speed at which each plane could be safely launched from an aircraft carrier.

Often, a carrier task force will encounter calm seas and no surface wind days during flight ops. Before the introduction of the steam catapults it was particularly important for the air boss to know the slowest safe speed he could catapult each airplane in each configuration because of the limited capabilities of the hydraulic catapults. Even after the installation of steam cats on upgraded carriers in the mid-1950s, along with the angled decks, the air boss remained acutely aware of minimum launching air speed requirements as the airplanes became bigger and heavier.

Frequently, in the era of the hydraulic catapults, the jets were launched at minimum safe speeds generated by the carrier going as fast as possible and the catapults launching at the maximum capacities, all of which were unnerving to the pilots. Once on a no-wind day during the Korean War, I was about to be launched in an F9F-2 from an H4B hydraulic catapult on the *Essex* when the catapult officer gave me a "hold" signal. I waited at idle as two ordinance men ran under my starboard wing and removed one of the four one-hundred pound bombs I was carrying. Then I was given a turn-up signal from the cat officer, followed by a launch signal and then a 150 foot ride down the catapult track. I staggered into the air wondering what would have happened if my plane had been one hundred pounds heavier. The answer, of course, is that it probably would not have made any difference. Later at Pax Riv, I became personally acquainted with the generation of minimums and realized that in my Korean launch incident, the air boss was just going "by the book" – a book generated by the Carrier Suitability test pilots of Pax River during carrier trials.

The Navy bureaucrats in Washington had a targeted minimum catapult end speed for each carrier-based airplane, which was all part of le grande task force plan for war. For example, they might show that a strike of four F9F-5 Panther jets could deliver four 250-pound bombs each on Wonsan if need be, with the only restriction being that each Panther had to be catapulted at 135 knots to stay out of the water. That was all on paper. We Carrier Suitability test pilots had to show that it could be done; if it could be done, that is. If our flight test results did not verify projections, there was unrest in the Bureau.

I did minimums in six flying machines while at Pax Riv: the AD-5N and AD-6 Skyraider, F7U-3 and F7U-3M Cutlass, the F9F-8 Cougar and the F11F Tiger Cat. Preparations for these tests were a bit hairy. Let me cite the F7U-3M as an example (see chapter 2). I needed to know the stall speed of this beast fully loaded and as close to sea level as possible since that is generally where the aircraft carriers would be located. So I would leap off the airfield at Pax using afterburner, climb to 1,000 feet in the take-off configuration, then fly it down to stall speed. Touchy. This speed would be the foundation for establishing the minimum safe launch speed for fleet pilots flying off aircraft carriers. Neither the Cutlass nor I had any interest in flying off the big boat at stall speed. In fact, I didn't even want to fly it at all, but who listens to a Lieutenant?

To establish a target minimum end speed for this machine based on the stall speed I had determined for a specific configuration, say 130 knots, the numbers players added up tolerances of catapult performance and wind speed measuring devices (anemometers) to determine a level for disaster. For example, if the catapult performance could not be controlled any closer than plus or minus three knots, the numbers boys gave me three more knots. If the anemometer was only accurate to plus or minus two knots, they gave me two more knots. Then they graciously gave me four knots for Marilynn and the kids, making my target end speed for minimum launch 130 + 3 + 2 + 4 =139 knots. There were no "gimmies" for pitching deck, gusty winds or lack of courage.

Aboard ship, the procedure for achieving the minimum safe end speed for the Cutlass in the referenced configuration was somewhat routine. I would be catapulted at 150 knots, then 144 knots, then finally at 139 knots if I felt comfortable in doing so. Thus, when I was poised for launch on the catapult, the signal to go came when the anemometer wiggled around a specific wind speed, the carrier bow was not pointed downward, and the catapult crew was back from lunch.

That figure of 139 knots then became sacrosanct as the minimum airspeed for launching the Cutlass in that specific configuration in fleet operations because it was acceptable for combat projections and had been verified by a Navy test pilot.

Before I arrived at Pax, the Carrier Suit boys had lost a pilot during minimums off the carrier when his plane stalled after the catapult shot and plunged into the Atlantic off Norfolk. Nothing came up. It was not a game and not to be taken lightly. Yet as my friend and super pilot Carl Cruse used to say, "You know you have a minimum when you come back aboard with water in the cockpit." He didn't say what color.

An interesting circumstance arose in our little group when I was doing carrier trials and minimums in the AD-5N off the *Coral Sea*. One of our lads was driving the F9F-8 Cougar doing the same kind of tests. The pilot's target minimum speed for a particular configuration was 132 knots, but something untoward happened during his launch at 142 knots enroute to his minimum scared him. Whether it was a sudden wind drop, pitching deck or whatever, he came back aboard and announced loud and clear that he was not flying that mother off the catapults a single knot slower than 142. This caused considerable unrest amongst our Navy white collar Washingtonians witnessing the operations from the Captain's roost.

I had flown the sweptwing F9F-6 Cougar and the F9F-7 (Flexdeck) but not the F9F-8. It was an upgraded version of the dash six with a modified wing and other newer stuff, but I had not been introduced to the latest from Grumman's Iron Works. Whilst I was sipping coffee in our ready room and explaining sex to a young j.g. about to be married, a small cadre of white shirts with ties approached, accompanied by my boss, Commander Bob Calland. Skipper graciously introduced me to the Bureaucrats and told them that he was sure I had flown the F9F-8 and would be pleased to continue the minimums program on this new machine after Hal had decided to cool it at 142 knots.

The white shirts explained that a minimum speed of 142 knots in this Cougar would severely curtail its usage in the fleet, thus jeopardizing the safety of the entire U. S. and A. It was sort of a motivational presentation which was appreciated and flattering to this young Lieutenant, but I advised them that they were talking to the wrong man because I had never flown the dash eight model.

"No worries" or words to that effect came from my CO. He allowed as how the F9F-8 flew much like its relatives, the dash six and dash seven Cougars, and that I would be catapulted at a nice safe speed, after which I could familiarize myself with the machine, feel out its stall characteristics, then return aboard to commence their version of the dash eight's minimum launch speed program from the carrier.

The familiarization flight was fun and "we" set up a plan for "my" program off the catapults. First launch at 145 knots was easy. Second launch at 140 knots, two below Hal's minimum, was not comfortable. The third launch at 135 knots was very shaky and produced two things: (1) Some water in the cockpit from within the flight suit; and (2) an irrevocable decision that I had made my last catapult launch in the dash eight Cougar in the quest for a lower minimum launch speed.

One rather abrasive and chunky white shirt with a poorly knotted bow tie allowed as how "we" needed to trim three more knots off the minimum launch speed attained so far. I volunteered to give him a cockpit checkout in the dash eight, and he could take the 132 knot cat shot, because I was not going to do it. He declined, of course, because (he said with a chuckle) he couldn't fly an airplane, but I believed it was because he couldn't swim.

After more than two years of that kind of flight testing, I agreed with some sage who said that flying minimums required the maximums in flying skills, whatever that means.

The catapulting of jet fighters and bombers off aircraft carriers is never routine. Fearless pilots and irascible catapult officers may make it look so, but it isn't.

I was sitting on the port catapult of the *Valley Forge* (CVA-10) in an F9F-5 ready for launch during the Korean conflict, with my wingman hooked up to the starboard cat. We were about to depart for a strike on Hamhung with six other fighters, carrying 250-pound bombs. He was to be launched first for reasons known only to catapult officers even if I was the glorious leader of this mission.

My wingman got the wind-up signal from the catapult officer, went to full thrust, checked his gages, then put his helmet against the headrest, saluted, and grabbed the stick for the 150-foot take-off run from the hydraulic catapult. Nothing happened. The cat officer then held his arms up crossed, meaning, "We're holding your launch," then pulled his arms back at his sides, which indicated to the pilot to throttle back to idle. He did. Moments later, with my wingman sitting at idle power, leaning on the cockpit rail, there was a sudden swoosh and down the deck went the F9F-5 Panther straight into the ocean.

Fortunately, the ship missed the sinking jet by the width of a paint job and the pilot bobbed to the surface cut and bruised but alive for a helo pick-up. Rotten way to start a mission.

Our squadron quickly devised a scheme to forevermore preclude inadvertent or premature cat shots, a methodology, however, summarily dismissed by the Naval air bureaucrats in Washington, who had never made a cat shot. We would provide a long thin rope at the catapult site on deck, one end of which would be handed to the pilot when he had positioned his jet on the catapult (canopy open for launch in those days). The other end of the rope ran down the outside the cockpit, across the deck to the catapult officer. There it would be attached to the catapult officer's personal parts and when the pilot was ready for launch, he would simply turn loose of his end of the rope.

A few years later, I was flying the F7U-3M Cutlass during carrier suitability trials on the *Shangri-la*. The -3M was hoisted aboard at North Island in San Diego as I was pushed up the gangway for the ordeal. The catapult officer had never seen a Cutlass, had not met me nor I him, and I sensed a cautious suspicion mutually shared as we prepared for carrier operations. So we negotiated and agreed to the signals we would use during launch operations and off we went.

The first two cat shots and landings were uneventful, at least as uneventful as they got in a Cutlass, and then it happened. I was hooked up on the starboard cat at full afterburner on both engines, ready for launch, when I got a "hold" signal from the cat officer. Then he gave me his throttle back signal, but it was not mine. I shook my head side-to-side indicating "nope." I'd told the cat officer that if he wanted me to throttle back in that airplane while it was hooked up to his catapult he'd have to walk out in front of it. Meanwhile with the afterburners scorching the deck, the captain on the bridge became convinced I was trying to burn his aircraft carrier to the waterline.

It all worked out okay. The catapult officer ran out in front of the Cutlass; I throttled back, and shortly afterward spent some tenuous moments on the bridge of the *Shangri-la* listening to the captain explain why he would be very pleased when I got that airplane and my ass off his ship.

From the carrier operations standpoint, all pilots and supporting crew strove for perfection for many good reasons – mostly centered around safety. Ideally, all landings would be on the centerline with the number three wire used for arrestment and all catapult launches would be made with the airplanes aligned perfectly on the catapult track. It doesn't always happen that way.

In carrier landings, a number of factors can cause a plane to land off center, pick up any one of the arresting cables or make free-flight engagements (wire pick-up prior to main gear touchdown). Landing aircraft sometimes miss the wires altogether, which is not a problem on angle deck carriers but was usually catastrophic in the days of straight deck carriers (Chapter One). Carrier planes are designed to accommodate the structural loads of most arrested landings no matter where the plane is landed on the deck. Most but not all.

In the catapult phase of carrier ops, planes may be launched with the main gear as much as six inches off the cat center line, but they are designed to accommodate such loads, and further, the launching parameters are much easier to control than those of landings.

Prior to the Navy accepting a new model airplane, a contractor civilian test pilot will have demonstrated in flight operations that there is sufficient strength in the machine to sustain the loads of less-than-optimum carrier landings and cat shots. Such demonstrations are performed at Pax Riv using the Test Center catapults and arresting gear with these tests being monitored by the Carrier Suitability engineering personnel and pilots.

Later on, after I became a civilian test pilot with Rockwell – then North American Aviation – I was involved in flying such structural demonstrations at Pax. As a Navy Lieutenant with Carrier Suit, I was one of our cadre responsible for evaluating the operational capabilities and limitations of the new model airplanes. For example, could the average fleet pilot safely control the airplane if it were catapulted from an off-center spot? Were the airplane's flying qualities adequate in a carrier approach to assure a safe landing on the carrier deck when made by the average fleet pilot?

In this evolutionary process, we Carrier Suitability test pilots flew programmed off-center arrested landings and catapult launches both ashore, at the Test Center, and then aboard aircraft carriers to assure that any airplane designed for fleet operations could fulfill its mission when flown by the average Navy pilot. I should say, however, it was my observation then and is now that there are few "average" pilots, male or female, flying off aircraft carriers. They are superior. They are the best in the world.

X

MACH 2

I spent seven wonderful years as an Engineering Test Pilot with North American Aviation, now Rockwell, in Columbus, Ohio. I was recently looking at a photograph taken of six NAA test pilots posing in front of an FJ-4 when I first joined the company. Only two are still alive, Ed Gillespie and I. The others were killed doing what they loved – testing airplanes. They were all exceptional pilots but something went wrong in the air and they died.

Our boss, who was not in the photograph, was Jim Pearce. Extraordinary man. He was a Navy Ace in World War II, became a test pilot with NAA and shortly thereafter lost his left leg below the knee to cancer. Didn't slow him up a bit. Now and then he would blow a tire during a landing rollout because he had little feel for the rudder pedal brakes – no ankle – but he never had an accident. Jim nailed a piece of two by four to the toe of his left shoe used in flight ops, and to depress the brake pedal he slid his two-by-foured shoe up onto the pedal and pumped the pedal with his knee. Not much feel, but it worked.

Once five of us, including Pearce, flew the company twin Beechcraft from Columbus to Pax River to attend a meeting of the Society of Experimental Test Pilots, to which we all belonged. George Burdick was designated the duty driver for the trip back to Columbus, and thus scarfed up Cokes as the rest of us cocktailed the evening away. Near departure time a phone call to Burdick, our duty driver, directed him to appear in Washington the next morning along with Georgie Hoskins and Bill Morse, leaving Moore and Pearce to drive the Beechcraft back to Columbus as midnight approached.

As Pearce and I climbed into the Beechcraft, he advised me that I was the pilot and he the co-pilot because I had more legs than he. I suspected that our collective blood/alcohol numbers were well into double digits, but off we went in the dark of night where later I made the best, smoothest landing at Columbus I'd ever made in a Beechcraft – ever. I generally did not land that airplane well. Who did?

Sometime later at a Test Pilots' Symposium convened at the Beverly Hills Hilton in Los Angeles, I was standing with three other test pilots, Jim Pearce, Nick Smith, and Smokey Yunick. Between the four of us, we had five legs. I had two of them. Smokey gave a leg to a helicopter, and Nick lost one from injuries incurred ejecting from an F3H-l Demon.

Jim Pearce is in the Test Pilots Hall of Fame as well he should be.

It is fun to recall that at the Test Pilot's Symposium previously mentioned, I was enjoying the banquet with more than two thousand others as we anticipated the appearance of Bob Hope as our master of ceremonies. The President of the Society of Experimental Test Pilots that year was – Jim Pearce, my boss. About halfway through the elegant dinner, Pearce showed up at the table where I was seated with my guests LaWanda and Morris Sievert of LaJolla, California. Jim advised me that Bob Hope had not appeared; they had not been able to contact him; they did not know where he was; and that if he did not show up, I was going to be the master of ceremonies!

Leaving the dinner table, I gathered with the program troops behind the podium to figure out what I was supposed to do. About ten minutes before T-zero, up walked Bob Hope as if everything were absolutely normal. I remember saying to him, "Bob, where the hell have you been?" And I remember his reply. He said, "Sonny boy, you're not old enough to know." The evening turned out great, no thanks to me. Thanks, Bob.

World famous aviatrix Jacqueline Cochran arrived in Columbus for a scheduled ride in the Vigilante, which had been arranged by the high muck-a-mucks in Washington. The objective, besides good public relations, was to get her to Mach 2 for the first time.

Jackie had flown past Mach 1 in North American's F-100 Super Sabre jet both as pilot of the machine and as a passenger in the two-seated version. Now it was on to Mach 2, she hoped. She was a great gal, strong willed and exceptionally knowledgeable in aviation matters, which came as no surprise to us test pilots at NAA who were pleased to associate with her in this venture. Her dominating personality deployed a wry sense of humor at all altitudes as I soon discovered.

We checked Jackie out in the rear seat of the A3J-1 Vigi. There were no flight controls in that cockpit, but she really did not care on this mission. She just wanted to achieve Mach 2. With the wisdom of a woman who held many aviation records, she carefully reviewed and digested cockpit matters related to safety – the ejection system, radios, and the like. But she was impatient and wanted to get on with it.

I was the lucky lad assigned to take this distinguished lady on her historic mission. The day was clear but the temperatures at altitude were unusually warm, which caused me some concern. At 35,000 feet, the temperature norm is minus 65 F degrees, but on this day, the weather man gave us a minus 56 F degrees reading, which would be marginal for attaining Mach 2. Our performance guys said it might be close, but I should make that speed okay with my precious cargo in the back seat. So off we went.

Our FAA assigned supersonic corridor stretched from Knoxville, Tennessee, to Columbus, Ohio, with the provision that we be subsonic over both cities. But for this mission I decided to get a head start on my northward run, and thus started over Gatlinburg, Tennessee, at 40,000 feet – and was at Mach 1.2 by the time we reached Knoxville. Sorry down there. Jackie asked some good questions as we motored northward and seemed delighted with the trip.

About Mach 1.6, our acceleration rate became noticeably slower as the Vigi engines struggled with the warmer air. At Mach 1.9, we were accelerating very slowly and I was running out of fuel and supersonic corridor at the same time. The Vigi stopped accelerating at Mach 1.96 as Columbus loomed close ahead. But I knew exactly what to do. I pushed the intercom button and said with pride, "Jackie, here we are at Mach 2." There was a moment's silence, then she replied, "Buster, you may be at Mach 2 in the front cockpit but I'm only at 1.96 in this cockpit."

Rats! I had forgotten that she had a Machmeter on the instrument panel in her cockpit. So it was out of afterburner and we returned to Columbus with the mission not accomplished. Jackie was pretty cute about telling our brass how much faster the front cockpit was than the rear one. She elected to stay another day to try it again with more optimum temperatures projected along with a faster pilot. So Jim Pearce saved the day by taking his elegant passenger to Mach 2.01 in both cockpits of the Vigilante at the same time.

*   *   *

Old axioms apply to new planes. One of my favorite and most dog-matic premises in cockpit layout when I had a voice in the evolution of new airplanes such as the Vigilante, the T-2B and C Buckeye trainers, and the OV-10 Bronco, was that the pilot must be able to see, reach and actuate every switch in the cockpit, day or night – not just most of the switches, but all of them. It goes without saying that he must know where they are and what they do; all part of training. It also goes without saying that not being able to locate or reach a particular switch in a particular circumstance could be fatal.

I was scheduled to make a post maintenance check flight in a Vigi-lante one morning after a thunderstorm had rinsed off all our flying ma-chines on the flight line at North American. It was supposed to be a routine flight but turned out to be something else, as often happens. Cleared for takeoff on Runway 27, I lit off afterburners and accelerated to lift-off speed. Immediately after sucking up the wheels the cockpit filled with fog. It was so thick I could see nothing. I could not see out; I could not see the gyro-horizon or anything on the instrument panel, nor could I see the console switches, or even the control stick. My immediate reaction was to try and jettison the canopy but my first action was to call the control tower about my major dilemma. The conversation went something like this (from the tower records).

"Columbus tower, I have an emergency. I can't see my instruments. Are my wings level?"

Tower: "Flight John, you are in a right bank, about thirty degrees. Roll left."

Flight John: "Roger. Tell me when level. What's my nose attitude?"

Tower: "Stop left roll. Wings are level. You are climbing too steeply. Nose her over. That's better. Hold it there."

By now I was out of afterburner and was being guided by the tower operator. Ahead lay downtown Columbus and the Ohio State University complex.

Tower: "Flight John, you are rolling into a right bank again. Roll your wings level. That's it. Hold it there."

By now I had located the cabin pressurization switch by feel and turned it off. Slowly, the instrument panel became visible, and I locked my unblinking eyeballs onto the gyro-horizon, which told me I was starting to roll right again.

I called the tower and told them my visibility was returning and I was okay, thanks to the very alert traffic controller on duty. I was at 3,000 feet, doing 280 knots directly over the Ohio State football stadium when I took over control of the aircraft from the tower operator. That afternoon I took him a bottle of Cutty Sark.

Postflight inspections of my Vigilante revealed that considerable water from a rainstorm had collected in the cockpit pressurization ducting, which produced the fogging. The system was redesigned, of course.

Sometime later, I had another encounter with a switch I could not locate. It almost cost me. We were developing an in-flight refueling capability with the A3J so that one, as tanker, could refuel a second, which could be carrying a nuclear weapon in a strike mode. The tests done in daylight indicated the system worked well and we determined that the pilot of the Vigilante taking on fuel with the probe and drogue scheme had more exacting longitudinal control of his plane with the pitch augmentation system turned off. The pitch aug switch was on the left console in back of the power control levers.

George Burdick, great test pilot, and I had the pleasure of being scheduled for the first evaluation of the refueling system at night – on a night which turned out to be very dark. I was to refuel from Burdick's Vigilante tanker, first at 20,000 feet, then at 30,000 feet over the Ohio countryside. My rear seat man was Andy Kendall, a bright and eager young engineer with not much flight experience but very able at his tasks in the rear seat. It would be a night he would long remember.

Burdick and I were in a loose formation climbing through 18,000 feet when I called him and advised that I was turning off pitch augmentation. Cockpit lighting was still being optimized, but I located the switch and turned it off. Immediately, the Vigilante began a pitch over to almost one negative G and full back stick had no effect whatsoever. I remember George saying, "John where'd you go?" No time to talk to George. The airplane continued to pitch over until we were in a vertical dive with full back stick meaning nothing to the stubborn machine. I had throttled back, thrown out speed brakes and ram air turbine, but we were still going straight down.

A major problem was that my seat belt had enough play in it to allow the negative G to plaster my helmet against the canopy a position from which I could not see nor locate the pitch aug switch to turn it back on. Andy, in the rear seat, had no idea what was happening except that he, too, was rattling around against the canopy.

It turned out not to be our night to die. Gradually, full back stick was initiating a recovery and we bottomed out of the dive at 2,800 feet indicated on the altimeter, which was about 2,000 feet above the ground, and at an indicated airspeed of 520 knots.

Since I seemed to be back in control, I radioed what had happened to George and to our flight test engineer in our control tower and further advised them I wasn't touching another cockpit switch and that, with any luck at all, I'd be landing in about fifteen minutes. The landing was uneventful.

Evaluation of the problem revealed that prior to my flight, a modified longitudinal control actuator had been installed in my plane, which had a characteristic completely unknown and unrecognized by our design and test engineers. To the horror of those concerned, they determined that when the pitch augmentation system was turned off by the switch in the cockpit, the horizontal stabilizers (slab tail) slowly went to full leading edge up, then just as slowly returned to the flight trim position regardless of control stick position. This resulted in the uncontrollable pitch down. Had I been able to see and reach the pitch aug switch to turn it on again, I could have regained control of the airplane.

Other than the scary part of the whole thing, I realized something important about myself. Through it all, it never occurred to me to bail out. I just did not think of that, and I am sure that if I had thought of it somewhere in the dive, I would have ejected myself and my rear seat man. I considered that to be a failing in my psyche and so advised my boss and our flight safety engineer, Bill Cahill, who flew with me frequently. I wanted them to know that if sometime I were found in a big hole in the ground surrounded by bent metal, the problem might well be that I simply did not think of bailing out .

The lighting was improved on both consoles of the Vigilante, the pitch aug switch was enlarged and I thereafter flew with my seat belt cinched down snugly. Also the "new" longitudinal control actuator was discarded. And on subsequent flights, we found that night refueling was duck soup. However, for some reason, Andy never would fly with me again at night.

On a personal note, when Andy and I returned to the readyroom that eventful night, our lovely little dark-eyed night clerk on duty who had been apprised of the in-flight trauma was in tears when we walked in and she gave each of us a big hug. I advised her I was off to the showers to cleanse the body of moistures which had accumulated thereon during that brief flight. Helen smiled then and said she would be up to wash my back. Fat chance.

Following my misadventure in the Vigilante that very dark night, when inadequate cockpit lighting precluded my finding the switch I needed, I got myself invited to the annual convention of the Aircraft Lighting Engineers Association, which convened in Pittsburgh. I was there to present a paper on the subject of cockpit lighting requirements as seen by the pilot who has some intrinsic interest in the subject. The following is the context of my message to the several hundred engineering gurus in attendance.

"It is the intent of this paper to review fundamental cockpit lighting requirements from the pilot's standpoint to the end that those who subject themselves to this presentation may regain personal contact with those of us who depend upon good cockpit lighting for the safety of our aircraft and ourselves during the hours of darkness.

The basic requirements for cockpit lighting are outlined below and subsequently discussed in the context of this presentation. They are:

1. The necessity for the pilot to see every switch and read every label in the cockpit;

2. The necessity for a minimum of canopy reflections;

3. Sufficient selectivity of lighting intensity for all conditions of darkness from dusk to dawn;

4. Satisfactory instrument panel and console lighting with no compromise to the pilot's night vision;

5. Even and equal light intensity for each instrument;

6. Soft lighting to avoid eye strain; and

7. Adequate intensity variation for warning lights for day and night operations.

Each of the above requirements will be discussed individually. The initial requirement that the pilot be able to see every switch and read every label in the cockpit cannot be compromised in any way. The modern cockpit of today's high-performance attack or fighter airplane is a maze of switches and instruments. It is almost redundant to state that no switch is included in the cockpit without a specific and important purpose. It is as important today as it was twenty years ago that every pilot flying an airplane know its cockpit by memory. Few pilots today, however, trust their memory implicitly in actuating any switch or control in the cockpit without visually ensuring that their fingers have selected the correct switch. The ease with which the pilot may see each switch and read its labeled function during daylight hours is taken for granted; its significance becomes manifest only at night if the pilot cannot clearly read the function of a specific switch, for this raises immediate doubt in his mind as to whether or not he has, in fact, located the switch he wants or needs. Too often, this doubt causes the pilot to grope for the flashlight dangling on a loose string about his neck for augmentation of his cockpit lighting. It may be stated simply that good lighting of most of the switches is not enough – every switch and its labeled function must be illuminated.

Pilots can live with canopy reflections of cockpit lighting much the same as they can live with grumpy wives or tw- year-old sports cars. The major objection to canopy reflections is that they vary with the position of the pilot's head, and thus are constantly changing with the pilot's change of head location or vision. The result is that the appearance and disappearance of reflections as perceived by the pilot's peripheral vision during motions of his head are distracting and highly undesirable. In connection with this, there is an old axiom which says that mid-air collision in the early morning hours will ruin your whole day. Thus, most pilots are constantly on the alert for perception of the running lights of airplanes during all hours of darkness. The distractions of canopy reflections from cockpit lighting are not only aggravating but can be weighed with a certain factor of safety.

Just as the evening twilight period provides problems of visibility for the automobile driver on the highway, this period is likewise a difficult one for the pilot in the cockpit. For the automobile driver, the most critical period of time is that segment of the evening when there is insufficient sunlight to make all objects along the roadside discernible, yet it is not dark enough for the headlights to be effective. During the same period in the air, there is insufficient daylight for the pilot to see his instruments and controls clearly, yet the console and instrument lights are inadequate. The cockpit lighting engineer must provide a wide variation in intensity for cockpit lighting to enable the pilot to cope with this critical lighting situation. As this particular period of the day approaches, the pilot usually turns all cockpit lights on to their brightest intensity, and as the daylight disappears and the pilot's dark adaptation takes place, he gradually reduces the intensity of the lights, often attaining the minimum illumination setting available as maximum darkness is reached.

Until complete automation has been accomplished in the control of take-off, cruise flight and landing, there will still be a need for the pilot to see out the windows of his airplane. The pilot's night vision, therefore, can in no way be compromised by the cockpit lighting. Much has been said in recent years about the pros and cons of white lighting for the pilot's cockpit. It can be substantiated by oculists and by flight physiologists that white lighting compromises a pilot's night vision by reducing his dark adaptation effectivity. Since the pilot cannot see what he cannot see, there is a tendency for a pilot, when his night vision is reduced, to proceed blithely on like a turtle with his head withdrawn, assuming that since has not run into anything yet, the chances are he will not. This does not necessarily promote safety of flight. Although positive control of all airplanes in congested areas at nighttime has become more prevalent, one need only take-off or land an airplane at the Washington National Airport to be keenly aware of the sensation that he closely resembles a bee departing from or returning to his hive. The importance of good night vision under these circumstances cannot be overstated.

The adverse effects of uneven instrument lighting, as with most lighting defects, are primarily psychological. One instrument, lighted slightly brighter than the others, is eye-catching to the pilot and after a period of time becomes like a thorn in the outer part of the retina, irritating and exasperating. To alleviate this condition, the pilot usually turns down the intensity of the brighter light until it is not discomforting, which results in other instruments being inadequately lighted. Unevenness of console lighting does not necessarily have the same undesirable effects upon the pilot unless the differences in intensities are gross, since his vision is concentrated primarily upon the instrument panel and the console lighting is at the extremes of his peripheral vision. It is interesting to note that a small but bright light on the instrument panel (if a shield were lost from a small bulb) usually becomes intolerable to a pilot after a short period of time. Invariably, such a circumstance is remedied one way or the other, by removal of the bulb, by covering the bulb with a torn segment of map, a piece of chewing gum, or by breaking the bulb. Hasn't civilization produced historic sadists who tortured captives by requiring them to look into bright sources of light? Surely, there are none of those among cockpit lighting engineers.

The solutions for correct lighting or correct presentation of warning lights in the cockpit are controversial, and in the present state of the art, not entirely satisfactory. Warning lights, as such, have two specific requirements insofar as their illumination characteristics are concerned. The first is that in daylight operations, the warning lights must have the ability to outshine the sun, and the second requirement is that at nighttime, the intensity of the light must be such that actuation of the light merely warns the pilot that something is amiss, but does not necessarily scare the hell out of him. To date, this pilot has not seen the warning light on the instrument panel the illumination of which is clearly discernible under all conditions of daylight lighting. Current warning lights in use have not attained their effectiveness because of their illumination capacity but because of their location on instrument panels in close proximity to instrument shrouds, which reduce the flight circumstances under which the sun shines directly on the lights. The overall effectiveness of the warning light system then still depends upon airplane attitude with respect to the sun. Quick to criticize, this pilot offers no concrete solution to the problem. It would seem that inherent improvement in warning indication systems using other than warning lights per se should be investigated more thoroughly. Since the eye is quick to detect motion, a moving needle or flag device would seem more appropriate as a master warning indicator than light bulb illumination, which, in spite of valiant efforts on the part of cockpit lighting engineers, cannot yet match the illumination capabilities of the sun.

There is an interesting aspect to the utilization of warning lights during night operations. Although it is conceded that the overall warning light illuminance should be reduced when cockpit lighting is selected for night operations, there is still a tendency to overilluminate warning lights on the premise that it is imperative the pilot not overlook the warning signals he is getting. On the other hand, illumination of a warning light at night usually portends trouble for the pilot. When the message has been delivered and he is aware of some specific trouble in his airplane, an extra bright warning light staring at him adds no solace or comfort. Bad news should be broken to a person gently and without fuss or dramatics.

There is one final point which should be made at this time. It is this: It is acknowledged that cockpit lighting today is an art and a science. Sufficient data has been accrued from doctors, flight physiologists, physicists, and from case histories to allow the lighting engineer to do a good job at lighting any given space. Armed with this knowledge, the cockpit lighting engineer can produce an artful job of illuminating a cockpit to meet almost any specification. Nonetheless, the artist/scientist/lighting engineer must subject the fruits of his work to the pilot for whom it is intended. How often has pilots' criticism of cockpit lighting mock-ups been countered by "that's merely his opinion"? "There are no scientific considerations in his comments and we can prove this cockpit lighting meets all specifications." It must be kept in mind that cockpit lighting is designed for the pilots who use it, not for the computers which calculate it.

In summary, the fundamental requirements for cockpit lighting as far as the pilot is concerned have not changed for several decades, nor are they apt to change in the future. The lighting engineer who can provide cockpit lighting which enables the pilot to see clearly every switch and read every label in the cockpit, with no loss of night vision to the pilot, without canopy reflections, with even light intensity for each instrument, with wide intensity variation, and with warning light intensities that outshine the sun, can be assured of job security unequaled outside the missile field."

Bright, personable, talented, great-looking and charismatic was Bud Holcomb. He could have been a movie star. Bud was the project test pilot assigned the FJ-4 Fury and was progressing smoothly through the flight test program in Columbus on schedule. The Navy, our customer, had sent an evaluation team of test pilots from Patuxent River to fly the FJ-4 and all agreed that Holcomb was doing his job well and that the Fury would be a fine addition to the Navy's carrier air groups.

Bud was doing build-ups in the flutter phase of the program; recording flight control dynamics on oscillographs installed in the nose of the Fury. No telemetry then.

The safety margin for potential flutter of the horizontal stabilizer was calculated to be an airspeed fifteen percent faster than the limit speed of the Fury as defined by the flight envelope. Holcomb had to demonstrate the validity of these engineering projections. All wind tunnel and flight test results up until the final data point, at limit airspeed, indicated no evidence of any flutter problems. To obtain the final data point, Bud rolled into a vertical dive, one hundred percent rpm called data on at 42,000 feet accelerating to limit mach number, which he expected to attain at 34,000. That was the last we heard from him.

Pieces of Holcomb's FJ-4 were scattered over a three-square-mile area south of Columbus. Enough of the oscillograph data was recovered to determine that the abruptness and severity of the Fury's disintegration meant that Bud was killed instantly when the cockpit section tumbled violently as flutter destroyed the horizontal stabilizer. The airplane had been slightly faster than limit speed and the flutter margin was not fifteen percent. We had lost a fine pilot.

The OV-10 Bronco project was assigned to Ed Gillespie. The OV-10 was a twin-engine turboprop light attack airplane that was being built for the Army and subsequently sold to many small countries worldwide as well. It had twin booms stretching aft with a vertical fin on each boom, and the horizontal stabilizer and elevator attached between the booms, much like the Lockheed P-38 Lightning configuration.

During Gillespie's flutter evaluation flights, data had indicated potential flutter problems as the airplane approached limit speed in the max "q" (maximum dynamic pressure) range of airspeeds, which could only be attained at very low altitudes because of mach number limits.

Redesign and strengthening of the horizontal stabilizer and elevator was accomplished on the Bronco, and flight data obtained by Gillespie during build-ups indicated the redesign was sound. The final data point to verify safe flutter margins was flown by our Chief Test Pilot, Dick Wenzell, because Ed was away on another mission. Wenzell was a superb technician as a test pilot: very exacting; very precise. He was one of the first members of the Society of Experimental Test Pilots to be elected a Fellow in the Society.

The data point Wenzell was to obtain would be at maximum or limit airspeed, which would be attained in a slight dive at an altitude below 500 feet. He would be accompanied by a chase pilot in a T-2C Buckeye jet trainer.

Dick was at the target airspeed, 450 feet above the ground when the horizontal stabilizer disintegrated. Before the chase pilot could yell "eject." Wenzell was out of the airplane. He had felt the control stick shake, followed by an uncontrollable pitch down. That gets the pilot's attention when he is in excess of 400 knots below 500 feet. He remembered grabbing the ejection ring and nothing more.

Wenzell's parachute deployed just before he hit the ground. Certainly it saved his life then, but he was badly broken up by the impact. His shoulders were separated, his eyes were extraordinarily hemorrhaged, he suffered major skull fractures and hemorrhaging in the brain. He had a broken arm and fractured pelvis. He was alive, but barely. Tragically, Dick never fully recovered from his injuries. The scarring of brain tissue caused his health and vitality to deteriorate until he finally succumbed in a nursing home in Columbus. Thus the demon flutter took the life of another great pilot and wonderful family man.

George Hoskins had as much talent as any test pilot who ever flew. He had flown with the Navy's Blue Angels flight demonstration team, flew jets in combat in Korea, then went to the Navy's Test Pilot School at Patuxent River. George and I were in Class 11 together, where we met.

At North American, Hoskins was a star. He was full of fun on the ground but one hundred percent serious in the air. Among his projects was the flight structural demonstration of the Vigilante – 5 G at Mach 2, 1.5 negative G at 1.4 Mach number, among other data points. Piece of cake, George would say.

We got a contract to install and evaluate a turboprop engine in the T-28 Trojan trainer. There wasn't much money in the contract, and Hoskins volunteered to fly the program without an ejection seat. Just the standard T-28 cockpit configuration. Tunnel tests were minimal so the flight evaluation program was limited in scope for reasons of safety. No terminal velocity dives, no rolling pullouts, no spins. Flight tests scheduled were mostly in the performance regime with an evaluation to be made of the general handling characteristics of the T-28 with the turboprop configuration. Piece of cake.

Hoskins reported that the plane handled nicely and was fun to fly. He had a data point scheduled for eighty percent of limit speed in a thirty degree dive at 10,000 feet. On this flight, he reported to the tower that he was pushing over at 15,000 feet, data on. That was his last transmission. Within an hour, a farmer reported to the police that a plane had crashed in a field near his house about thirty miles southeast of Columbus. It was George's T-28. He was still in the cockpit. The entire tail section had twisted off his airplane, attributable to the loads imposed by the prop wash flow from the turbo engine propeller.

The canopy was open about six inches and there were well defined marks on the leading edge of the canopy, which came from George's knee pad. When the tail twisted off, the fuselage was twisted and the canopy rails bent to the extent that George could not get the canopy open. As he was tumbling down in the T-28, he was trying to pry the canopy open with his knee pad so he could bail out. With no ejection seat, he was doomed. What a loss to the aviation world and his family and us.

At Columbus, we were grinding out production models of the F-100D, which were flown out by our production test pilots when they came out of manufacturing. When the new 100s had performed scheduled tests in flight as verified by our production pilots, they were turned over to the military pilots stationed in Columbus. When the Navy or Air Force pilots were satisfied that the new production planes were manufactured as designed and flew as advertised, the military would accept the airplanes and North American would get paid.

As an engineering test pilot, I had not flown the F-100 because there was no occasion for or reason to get into the machine. The production guys did all that stuff with new airplanes. On a bright afternoon, however, I was invited to fill in and help out the production pilots. It seemed that a new 100 had been rolled out the door, fueled, checked and prepped for its first flight, but the production cadre did not have a pilot available to fly it. Let's let John do it.

After reviewing the procedures I was to follow in this first flight of this F-100D and getting a cockpit checkout, it was into the blue with an afterburner take-off. It was a nice flying airplane and I was soon level at 40,000 feet with all systems go. One of the first maneuvers on the checklist was a three G turn at Mach 1. The Super Sabre accelerated smoothly in afterburner to the desired mach number and I rolled into a three G turn. Just as I hit three G there was a terrific "bang" that seemed to be right under the cockpit. It scared the wits out of me. I immediately came out of afterburner and leveled out. All the gauges read normal, but it took me a little while to return myself to normal. The engineering troops and I conferred via radio, and we concluded it was probably a compressor stall and that "we" should continue the flight. Easy for them to say from their air-conditioned offices. As far as I was concerned, it was a "next pilot check."

The last test to be made on this flight was that of the auto labs system. The airplane was capable of releasing some potent bombs in a number of modes including the labs or loft maneuver, which involved a high-speed, low-altitude run-in toward a target with the pilot pulling up at three to four G into an Immelman for his escape. The bomb or bombs would be released at about the forty-five degree point in the pull-up. This airplane had an auto labs system wherein the entire maneuver could be accomplished by the autopilot, including the bomb release and the roll-out at the top of the maneuver.

And so it was off to 500 knots at 5,000 feet with the system set up for the venture. I pressed the button to start the pull-up and the F-100 immediately rolled inverted and headed for the ground. Wrong. The system apparently had decided to do the maneuver backward and was starting with the roll-out, at the bottom instead of the top. Of course, I took over and rolled out and pulled up safely, but it was a bit hairy for a moment. I added an asterisk to the "next pilot check."

The F-100 was not yet through with me and seemed determined to make my first flight in it a memorable one. The landing loomed ahead on Columbus' 8,000-foot runway which would normally be ample for the 100 if everything worked right and was done right. The Super Sabre had a drag 'chute and non-skid brakes to help stop the plane during landing roll-out. I had never flown either of those systems before and looked forward to seeing how they worked.

Touch-down at about 140 knots was smooth (naturally), and I quickly deployed the drag 'chute but didn't feel anything. The control tower called, "Flight John, your drag 'chute detached and is lying on the runway." They do work better when they are attached to the airplane. It is surprising how quickly 8,000 feet of runway is used up at 140 knots. As I depressed the brake pedals hard, I thought the non-skid system had better work or I'd end up in the end-zone of Ohio State's football stadium. Thank God that system functioned and I got stopped okay but not comfortably.

My respect for the production test pilots was significantly enhanced by my first flight in the F-100, and I was glad to return to the safety of engineering flight testing.

The A3J-l Vigilante was designed as a Mach 2 attack bomber capable of delivering the world's most powerful nuclear weapons to any target anywhere. From its linear bomb bay, positioned between the two J-79 engines, a hydrogen bomb could be ejected aft out of the tail at speeds up to Mach 2. No bomb bay doors to open, no induced drag during bomb release. Neat.

The rocket scientists got together with our engineering gang at North American to produce an interesting hypothesis. They concluded that with a rocket boost, the Vigilante might be able to make a run-in toward a target at Mach 2, 45,000 feet and at *le momente critique* the pilot could light off the rocket located at the base of the vertical fin, and climb the Vigi to some altitude above 70,000 feet still at Mach 2 for release of its nuclear weapon. There were a number of tactical advantages to this scheme, not the least of which was safety of plane and crew.

A prototype of the liquid rocket engine and its associated equipment was installed at the base of the vertical fin of an FJ-4 Fury, which was then designated the FJ-4F. It was one-of-a-kind and I was designated its one-of-a-kind rocket test pilot. This was in 1957 and there weren't many pilots around driving rocket-powered airplanes, but with a stroke of our chief test pilot's pen, I became one.

The FJ-4F incorporated some significant modifications to accommodate the rocket engine. The most noticeable to the pilot was the jet engine tail pipe, which was expanded ten percent in area in hopes that the jet engine would neither flame out nor over-temp at altitudes above 70,000 feet during the flight tests. This resulted in a significant reduction in the thrust available for take-off and climb-out. A second modification was the installation of a hydrogen peroxide fuel tank, which they located directly below the pilot's seat. Since hydrogen peroxide can go unstable rather quickly under certain circumstances, the very funny joke amongst the test engineers was that if instability occurred in flight that resulted in an explosion, the pilot would be the first to know. Very funny.

I was launched via Delta Airlines to Boston for a visit with the David Clark Manufacturing Company located on the outskirts of town. The Company made partial pressure flight suits for test pilots like Chuck Yeager and Scott Crossfield, who were plying their trade at altitudes above 60,000 feet. At this altitude an engine or cockpit pressurization failure would likely be fatal to the pilot unless he was wearing either a full pressure or partial pressure suit, such as manufactured by the David Clark team.

The visit to this firm was interesting and fun, for besides making pressure suits, they also made brassieres for Sears Roebuck retail stores. So for the personalized partial pressure suit they would make for me, I was literally measured from stem to stern. I asked that they make a particular measurement for me using their expertise and learned from this, should I need it, I would wear a 39 triple "A" brassiere.

On my third visit to David Clark for a final pressure suit fitting, they offered to nicely package a brassiere for my wife as a personal gift from them. I told them Marilynn's size and they said, "Take this one. She will love you for it." Marilynn unwrapped it and was delighted. It was a 38 "D" – about two sizes too big – but she was truly pleased in believing that was how I remembered her when I was away. She loved me for it.

The pressure suit with me in it was checked out in the pressure chambers at the Wright-Patterson Air Force Base test facility in Ohio. It performed as designed at 50,000 feet simulated altitude although my mobility was severely inhibited with the suit inflated, particularly in hand and finger dexterity. I hoped I would not have to fly the FJ-4F with the suit pressurized.

I made five flights in the modified Fury with the rocket engine pushing me to almost 80,000 feet but not without some graying of hair.

On the first flight, with a chase plane flown by Ed Gillespie filming the rocket engine light-off at 41,000 feet, the highest I could get with my modified jet engine, all went well except I did not set up the instrumentation data recording quite right, causing no joy in Engineeringville. Max altitude reached – 71,000 feet. Jet engine did not flame out, though tail pipe temperatures were near limit. Everyone happy but engineering. During the second flight I flew the -4F to stall, which occurred at 130 knots indicated airspeed at 74,000 feet. I was astounded to read the mach number. It was Mach 1.2 at my stall speed. Engine temps were marginal.

On the third flight, rocket light-off occurred at 42,000 feet (cold day), and all went well to almost stall speed at 75,000 feet when the jet engine tail pipe temperature reached red-line. I pulled the power control lever back rapidly. Wrong. The jet engine flamed out, the cockpit pressure indicator went berserk, and in moments I was a glider at 70,000 feet with my partial pressure suit fully inflated. I could not grip the control stick with rigid fingers but that was not a problem because I could drive the plane with the palm of my right hand on the top of the stick. It was a long glide down to 20,000 feet for an air start, where the sweet big-tail-piped engine lit off nicely, and it was on to home base. I was pleased when the pressure suit relaxed.

On the fourth trip, I was asked by the aerodynamic boys to evaluate the potential for adverse inertial coupling effects at maximum altitude for the flight, which turned out to be 75,000 feet. I had no idea what to expect but the aero guys thought the plane would probably tumble. Turned out the Fury performed brilliantly in a full aileron 360 degree roll at that unlikely altitude, at idle power, which was ninety-two percent rpm, and it was home again.

Prior to my last flight I was asked about how the sky looked when I was at 75,000 feet. What color was it? Could I see the curvature of the earth? The answer was: I had no idea. I had not looked out of the cockpit to everyone's amazement, including mine. So on my last flight, designed to attain the maximum altitude possible, I instructed my test engineer in our control tower to remind me to look "out the window" when I got there.
We had favorable temperatures enabling me to light off the rocket engine at 43,500 feet. Peak altitude was just under 80,000 feet. Jet engine at idle, ninety-six percent rpm. The word came. "John, look out of the cockpit." Above me the sky was a very deep blue. It phased into a lighter blue toward the horizon and a small white band sat just above earth, which was the haze level. Not many pilots back then had been privileged to see this beautiful version of the sky which has become commonplace to those in space exploration. To me it was elegance, and I felt privileged to witness these surreal colors surrounding me in the heavens. But I could not see the curvature of the earth.

The rocket boost evaluation program was concluded. The decision was made, however, not to install a rocket booster system in the Vigilante, inasmuch as a plan evolved to convert it into a state-of-the-art reconnaissance airplane, the RA-5C, which subsequently did yeoman service in VietNam.

My partial pressure suit, one of only a few made, is now on display in the San Diego Aerospace Museum. It looks great there.

*   *   *

North American was developing a new jet trainer for Naval aviation when I joined the company in 1956. It was designated the T-2J and called the Buckeye. Originally a single jet, two-seats-in-tandem machine, the jet engines caught up with the cockpits and it became the T-2C twin jet intermediate trainer, still called the Buckeye, and is still in service today. The airplane has enabled thousands of aviation cadets to learn about flying jet airplanes and how to land on aircraft carriers.

At North American Aviation, I was designated the project test pilot for this delightful machine, which proved to be a tough little creature and a blast to fly. I also learned about some of the machinations of the Navy project office in Washington that oversaw the development and flight demonstrations of the Buckeye.

Navy pilots driving military airplanes are unaware of the extent of flight testing performed on the planes prior to their being assigned to fleet or training squadrons. Service pilots know how to fly the plane they are in, how fast and high it will go, its G limits, stall speeds, and general flying characteristics. But the Navy project administrators will not accept a new model airplane, such as the Buckeye trainer, until the manufacturer's test pilots have demonstrated in flight that it will successfully meet all its design parameters. These include strength (the Vn envelope), speed, ceilings, spin characteristics, and take-off and landing distances, among other design criteria.

In the Buckeye, for example, I had to demonstrate flame-out landings in two configurations: (1) Engines shut down but windmilling; and (2) engines shut down and simulated frozen, i.e., zero rpm. After I successfully completed these flame-out landing tests at Columbus, the Navy stipulated in the trainer's handbook: DO NOT ATTEMPT TO LAND THIS AIRPLANE WITH THE ENGINES FLAMED OUT. IF THE ENGINES ARE NOT OPERATING THE CREW IS TO EJECT FROM THE AIRPLANE. Actually, the Buckeye handled very nicely in flame-out landings, but I could understand the reticence of training command administrators in having student pilots attempting this maneuver.

The T-2C Buckeye was a 7.5 G airplane when flown without tip tanks and a 6.0 G airplane with tip tanks installed. The Navy never flew the Buckeye without tip tanks but I did for months, demonstrating its flight structural envelope at 7.5 G. For instance, the airplane was designed to withstand

7.5 G at its limit speed, 485 knots, both at maximum aft center of gravity and limit forward c.g. To demonstrate the Positive Low Angle of Attack (PLAA) data point, I had to accelerate the Buckeye to 510 knots in a 30 degree dive – that's 25 knots beyond its limit speed – then pull back on the stick with both hands as hard as I could to achieve 7.5 G at 485 knots at the aft c.g. location. The excess 25 knots was needed because I lost that much speed to induced drag in the pull-up. Altitude, as I bottomed out, was 2,500 feet, not much if something broke. The worst maneuver I had to demonstrate, however, was 7.5 G at 300 knots Positive High Angle of Attack (PHAA), the upper left hand corner of the Vn envelope, where the poor old Buckeye stalled violently at exactly 300 knots, 7.5 G. It was an awful thing to do to an airplane – any airplane.

In trying to demonstrate the PHAA maneuver, the first attempt wrinkled the horizontal stabilizer. That was fixed, sort of. During the second attempt, most of the right-side horizontal stabilizer and elevator broke off and fluttered to a soft landing in a farmer's field. I made a hard landing at Columbus. Finally, engineering got it right and I accomplished the PHAA maneuver satisfactorily.

Unfortunately, with the modified horizontal stabilizer in place, I had to repeat the high speed PLAA 7.5 G maneuvers – back to an uncomfortable 510 knots in the little machine. I should mention that with the T-2C at its limit forward c.g., I was not strong enough to pull 7.5 G and had to achieve that data point using nose-up trim in the maneuvers. Terrible thing to do, but it worked.

Another ugly maneuver was the negative G data point which was to be demonstrated at negative 2.5 G, 400 knots. Achieving the negative G value was not as much of a problem as how the maneuver was to be done. I had to apply at least 60 pounds of push force on the control stick in less than .3 second, then hold that force until the negative 2.5 G was reached. I could not do this maneuver with the standard Buckeye seat and shoulder restraining harness because I could not get it snug enough, so I had a separate seat belt installed just to hold me tightly enough in the seat to achieve this crazy data point.

Then there were the spin demonstrations where the requirement was that I hold pro spin controls until the Buckeye had completed five complete turns before applying recover controls. And then the flame-out test wherein

I was required to roll the Buckeye inverted at 38,000 feet and fly inverted until the engines flamed out. At flame-out, I lost cockpit pressurization, of course, accompanied by frosting of the canopy and windscreen. But it was pretty quiet up there. I lit the engine again at 25,000 feet with the return of pressurization and the ability to see out the window again.

The gambit was that I had to achieve all the required structural and aerodynamic data points in the Buckeye in a carefully scheduled build-up program at Columbus and then take the plane to the Naval Air Test Center to repeat each data point under the scrutiny of Navy Flight Test personnel both in the air and on the ground. All went well in the flight demonstration program, and the Buckeye went on to become a favorite and a workhorse in the training command.

My tasks in helping develop and demonstrate the Buckeye trainer paled by comparison to George Hoskins' similar responsibilities with the RA-5C Vigilante. Georgie, the consummate test pilot, made it look easy and made the Vigi look great. Five G at Mach 2; negative 1.5 G at Mach 1.4; 4 G rolling pull-outs at supersonic speeds. Wow. And nobody in his right mind would have done a spin program in the Vigi – upright and inverted five-turn spins yet. But Zeke Hopkins did it. George Burdick successfully ejected a simulated nuclear weapon out of the Vigi's linear bomb bay at Mach 2, at 40,000 feet. In demonstration of the aircraft's seat ejection system, I fired an anthropomorphic dummy out of the back seat at 100 knots rolling down the runway at Columbus. Scared the wits out of me. Ed Gillespie fired a dummy out of the rear seat at 500 knots over the Pax Riv ordinance range. Scared the wits out of him. A cockpit suddenly full of flames and smoke from the ejection rocket is an attention getter. Both tests were successful.

In the course of my years as a test pilot with North American, I believe I flew some of the best airplanes in the world and some of the worst. The great ones included the Vigilante, the Buckeye, and the FJ-4 Fury series. Two of the worst ones were the McDonnell F-101 Voodoo, which we brought aboard to chase the Vigilante early in its development, and the North American AJ-1 Savage, which we resurrected as a flying electronics laboratory for the development of some of the Vigi's electronic systems.

The F-101 flew as if it had no wings at all, which may have partly accounted for the stick-snatcher installed in the cockpit that would snatch the control stick out of the pilot's hand at the onset of an uncontrolled pitch-up, an event that could occur in a turn. The AJ was powered by two Pratt and Whitney R-2800 reciprocal engines and one Allison J-33 jet engine, which was mounted in its belly. I finally had the privilege of flying this machine from Columbus to Scottsdale, Arizona, where it took its rightful place in the airplane graveyard.

In the last two years of my test pilot tenure at NAA, I was awarded a second hat – that of Chief, Flight Test Project Group – to go along with my responsibilities as test pilot. The added administrative duties were helpful in the learning process and certainly instrumental in my climbing out of the cockpit at the age of forty to become Apollo Test Operations Manager at the Kennedy Space Center for North American Aviation. And so in 1963, it was good-bye Ohio, hello Florida.

XI

DEATH ON PAD 34

The Challenger tragedy was Apollo One revisited. The death of Gus Grissom, Ed White, and Roger Chaffee in the 1967 Apollo One Command Module fire on Launching Pad 34 at the Kennedy Space Center rocked the nation. It was not just the loss of three heroes, three skilled test pilots, three devoted family men, but a tragedy which could have been avoided.

I was Manager of the Apollo Test Operations for North American Aviation at the Kennedy Space Center, responsible for organizing and supervising the NAA test team and responsible to the National Aeronautics and Space Administration (NASA) for Apollo spacecraft checkout and launch operations. It is important to emphasize that all test and launch operations were and still are totally under control of NASA. As in the Challenger tragedy, NASA personnel made all the decisions related to go-no-go, launch-don't-launch.

After my years as an engineering test pilot with management experience, it was a logical progression for me to go from the cockpit to a management position in a space flight program where there were men in the loop. The astronauts were appreciative of this approach and very comfortable with it.

The three astronauts died because they were trapped when a fire started in the command module, unable to open the hatch because of pressure build-up. The hatch opened to the INSIDE! North American's original design of the command module had the astronauts' hatch opening to the outside specifically to provide an escape avenue for the astronauts in the event of problems which might occur during the test and checkout phase of the spacecraft prior to launch.

189

After the contract for the command and service modules was awarded to North American, NASA issued one of its first contract changes, specifying that the hatch of the command module be redesigned to open INWARD instead of OUTWARD – a fatal decision.

Just prior to the tragic test, I met with Gus Grissom on behalf of my test team – one test pilot talking with another – to advise against proceeding until a more thorough review could be made of the test data accumulated to that point. My boss, another test pilot, met with Gus and Ed White the night before the test to again explain our position against proceeding. Gus took our advice to NASA management, which decided our reasons were not good enough to stop the test. The three astronauts died the next evening, January 27, 1967. Their bodies were found on the inside of the burned-out command module, at the hatch they could not open.

The Challenger tragedy followed when NASA proceeded to launch the shuttle against the advice of its contractor personnel.

Early in 1963, I arrived at Cape Canaveral as Apollo Test Operations Manager for North American, which was under contract to build the Apollo command module, service module, and launch escape system. A nucleus of our test team was in place consisting of bright young test engineers who had supported some of North American's projects at the Cape, such as the Navaho and other unmanned flight hardware.

Without question it was a learning process for us. NASA had in place an experienced team, which had launched the Mercury and Gemini spacecraft. We were accountable to those talented individuals for testing and launching Apollo, first from the Pad 34 launch complex, then Pad 39 at the Kennedy Space Center which at that time was under construction across the Banana River from the Cape Canaveral launch sites.

The procedures by which we operated were NASA's: rigid and intransigent. For example, one morning a North American technician noticed one of four tires on a small mobile trailer needed air and he started to inflate the tire but was abruptly stopped by NASA inspectors because he had no approved work order to do the job. The paperwork for pumping up the tire required authorizing signatures from three North American engineers and three NASA engineers. Paperwork in hand, the technician then pumped up the tire; the work being observed, inspected, and signed-off by one each North

American and NASA inspector. We wondered if we would need a work order to go to the bathroom and how many inspectors would monitor that function.

Somehow we managed to bring to the Cape, checkout, and launch, a command module into a suborbital trajectory using this scheme, which must have required two million signatures of approval and authorization. The command module with its parachutes did its thing, and how do you knock success?

The management chain-of-command was mind-boggling for me. I was employed by North American Aviation and accountable to them. I was also accountable to and under the direction of NASA personnel at the Kennedy Space Center. As far as they were concerned, I worked for them. But the program control was at NASA Houston whose people controlled the budget and thus my manpower levels. Sometimes I wondered if NASA's Houston and Kennedy Space Centers were working on the same program.

As an example, North American was providing engineer and technician services during the activation of the operations and checkout building, the parachute packing building, the command module/service module mating facility, the vehicle assembly building and the launch pad complexes, all of which included an inordinate amount of ground support equipment. I projected it would require 115 technicians for those tasks – the NASA Houston guy said we needed only twenty-three. I wondered if he had ever been to the Cape, so I went to Houston to see him and his staff. He stuck with twenty-three technicians, so I invited him to the Cape for a look-see. I took him up to the top of the launch tower at Pad 34 and out onto a catwalk where he could look out and down – and see forevermore. Nothing like a little acrophobia to focus the mind. I got more technicians.

The problems of being accountable to the various entities only compounded the tasks of readying spacecraft and facilities for launch operations. In addition, various segments of the Apollo testing program were managed by some men with the strongest wills in the business:

Scott Crossfield, North American Aviation, X-15 pilot, super engineer, a will of steel. We would do it his way.

Jim Pearce, North American Aviation, Test Pilot's Hall of Fame. As they say, he didn't get there by accident. We would do it his way.

Joe Shea, Max Faget and Chris Craft, National Aeronautics and Space Administration, Houston. They had supervised the manufacturing and launching of most of the spacecraft which had flown. We would do it their way.

Rocco Patrone and George Page, National Aeronautics and Space Administration, Kennedy Space Center. They had successfully launched Mercury and Gemini spacecraft. We would do it their way.

We were doing it Rocco's way on Apollo One.

There have been some very excellent books and articles written about the Apollo One fire; some by the astronauts who were closest to the crew who died, some by aviation historians, and one exceptional book by the Grissom family pastor, educator and researcher; all accurate and with a common thread – it should not have happened.

There were many factors contributing to the tragedy and many fingers pointed at engineers, testers, quality control, schedules. Yes, schedules. Too many problems put on back burners because of the need to "stay on schedule." We had a lunar landing to make before the year 1970, so schedule was sacrosanct. We at North American were engineering the space vehicle even as we were doing final tests on it. Even as the integrated systems test, the one in which the crew perished, was being run there were as many as a hundred engineering work orders outstanding on the command module. Joe Shea said there were more than 200 failures of one kind or another logged during tests of the spacecraft prior to this test. Why did we press on? Schedule.

In my mind one of the major contributing factors resulting in the loss of Apollo One's crew was the design of the command module hatch. It was originally planned to open outward, the premise being that in the event of a mishap during ground checkout, the crew would have an escape avenue available. Just open the hatch and get out of the command module into the safety of the white room. NASA's project management, however, was more concerned about the hatch being properly sealed during space flight and the necessity to preclude accidental hatch opening in space which would be fatal. Consequently, the hatch was redesigned to open inward so the oxygen pressure of about 5 psi in flight would seal it shut. It did. Even under ideal conditions it took approximately five minutes to open that hatch inward. From the moment the fire started there was no way to open the hatch for escape. Gus, Ed, and Roger were doomed.

As we at Kennedy Space Center (KSC) approached the "plugs out" integrated systems test, my test team was concerned about going from one test to another without analyzing reams of oscillograph data taken during previous tests. Test results for the monitoring engineers then were in real-time CRT's (cathode ray tubes or television screens) and also oscillograph data, which took time to analyze but was necessary in looking for trends. We did not have time to look for trends. I expressed this concern to Gus Grissom the day before the test and my boss, Jim Pearce, did the same thing the evening before the fatal test, talking at length to both Gus and Ed White about moving ahead without knowing for sure where we had been. Test pilots talking to test pilots. Gus expressed our concerns to KSC project management. Wally Shirra was concerned, too, and did not feel comfortable with the planned integrated systems test scheduled. Gus had to agree with his management that no one could give specific reasons for not going on – and so they did.

Subsequent exhaustive review of oscillograph data failed to reveal the cause of the fire but did show some trends that would have caused enough concern for us to look at some things inside the spacecraft, which *might have* – that is *might have* been helpful. Hindsight.

Few of those involved considered the possibilities of fire on the ground. Almost everyone was comfortable with the pure oxygen environment, even at 5 psi in the spacecraft. One North American Aviation scientist, Frank Hendel, in 1964, specifically pointed out to NASA in a formal report the fire hazard in a pure oxygen environment. He stated that the use of 100 percent oxygen at 14.7 pounds per square inch or more presents a fire hazard which could be especially devastating on the launch pad. But NASA had experienced no problems with this environment in Mercury and Gemini. Why now?

A factor overlooked – NASA had allowed the installation of an inordinate amount of hydrocarbon materials into the command module interior, velcro and nylon for example, both flammable. No problem if there is no fire. And what's to start a fire? Hindsight.

Many, many changes and improvements occurred as a result of this tragedy. One of the changes was the hatch. It was redesigned again to open outward and could be opened in less than ten seconds.

*　　　　*　　　　*

There were plenty of apprehensions among the testers, the crew, the technicians and everyone associated with the scheduled integrated systems test, called "plugs out" – not that anyone expected anything bad to happen. It was more that we were not confident about how the command module would perform in this complicated test.

As said before, the spacecraft was not in good shape considering it was only a month away from launch. One could feel the tension as the three astronauts prepared to enter the command module at 11:00 a.m., January 27, 1967. But there were nagging delays from the beginning and it was after 1:00 p.m. when the crew finally got into the spacecraft in their cumbersome space suits. From the start, there were communication problems with static drowning out voice transmissions. At one point, Grissom was heard to say, "How the hell can you hear me from the moon if you can't hear me five miles away?"

Wally Shirra was particularly concerned about "plugs out" and told Gus that if he encountered any problems during the test he should just call it off and get the hell out of the spacecraft. When the communications problem arose, Wally felt it was time to stop and regroup. But the test went on.

After the cabin had been pressurized to 2 psi above atmospheric pressure, i.e., 16.7 psia, in 100 percent oxygen and the test was underway, Grissom smelled a peculiar odor in the spacecraft and the countdown went to the hold mode as technicians tried to determine its source. They could find nothing wrong, so the test resumed.

At 6:31 p.m., a voice came from the spacecraft: "Fire – we have a fire in the spacecraft." Subsequently, I listened to the tape of that voice, or those voices, countless times, the fateful message lasting about fifteen seconds. It was garbled and there was not much agreement among the listeners as to exactly what was said or whose voice it was. I believed it to be Roger Chaffee and this is what I heard:

"Fire."

"We've got a fire in the spacecraft."

"We've got a bad fire – we're getting out."

"We're burning up ..."

Then ... a piercing scream lasting perhaps two seconds.

That was all.

The inside of the spacecraft had become an inferno and the three astronauts died within seconds after the blaze started. A spark had ignited the myriad combustibles in a 100 percent oxygen environment under two pounds of pressure, generating temperatures in excess of 1,000 degrees F. They didn't have a chance. From where the bodies were found, it appeared Ed White had been trying to open the hatch and Grissom was trying to help. Cameras focussed on the hatch window confirmed the astronauts' futile efforts to open a hatch that could not be opened.

Within seconds after the fire was reported, the spacecraft ruptured from the intense internal pressure and the fire blew itself out. As has been reported many times by many sources, the inside of the command module was devastated by the holocaust to the extent that the source of the fire was never precisely defined or identified.

I think Frank Borman, astronaut and subsequent commander of Apollo Eight, expressed the feelings of all involved after seeing the carnage the following morning when he said he could hardly begin to describe the chamber of horror encountered as he entered that burned spacecraft.

Frank had flown in from Houston in a T-38 and was the first person to crawl into the charred wreckage after the bodies of Gus, Ed, and Roger had been removed. He reported that it was a charred shell which was not a recognizable facsimile of a spacecraft. He was overwhelmed with the disaster, with three superbly trained test pilots having died – having been trapped in a supposedly routine ground test which was not even considered hazardous.

All of Frank's sentiments reminded me of an old test pilot adage, which avers there is no such thing as a routine test flight. They are all hazardous. Case in point: Three fine test pilots had died in a motionless spacecraft parked safely on a launch pad doing a routine, non-hazardous test. Of course, there is no such thing.

It took little time for everyone associated with the Apollo program to feel inadequacy and shame for not having done better. There was blame enough for everyone – North American Aviation for inferior workmanship, NASA for its complex and bloated management arsenal, the testers for allowing things to go too fast, the astronauts for their willingness to tolerate questionable designs and hardware. They would never have done that testing airplanes. We all contributed to the tragedy.

Walt Cunningham, back-up crew member for Apollo One, probably said it best in a speech at the Cape when he said, in effect, that the investigation became an incrimination of everyone connected with Apollo, including those who were to fly it. He pointed out the astronauts' failings by their willingness to tolerate questionable designs, equipment, and test procedures and by ignoring their own good sense of flight testing. Walt added that the astronauts believed many things needed changing but changes meant delays, which program managers wanted avidly to avoid. It was his belief that NASA program management and contractors alike were on a different frequency with the flight crew. There were too many disciplines going in too many different directions, Walt said. Anyone who ever flight tested an airplane would surely agree with Walt's sentiments.

The next command module in line had been essentially completed and was being readied for shipment to the Cape when the fire occurred on Pad 34. The inspectors, NASA and NAA, who had already accepted this vehicle and had proclaimed it ready to go, were ordered back into the spacecraft for a second look after the fire destroyed Apollo One. And some second look it was. They wrote up more than 1,500 discrepancies in the wiring harnesses after having initially proclaimed them ready for flight. The wake-up alarm had sounded for every man and woman in the program – every company president, NASA director, program manager, engineer, astronaut, inspector, tester – everyone. It was about time. And what a price to pay for a wake-up call.

Frank Borman, a bright, personable man, was a key person in the Accident Review Board examining the Apollo One disaster. He was one of the head coordinators of the twenty-one panels and 1,500 experts involved in determining what caused the Apollo One fire. I was involved with the initial Accident Review Assessment Team as Borman's counterpart, representing North American but was soon replaced by management types much further up the ladder than I. Borman was a class act in a most difficult and trying circumstance.

The Review Board presented its findings to the Senate Space Committee on April 11, 1967, and they were published by the U.S. Government Printing Office as "Apollo Accident, Hearing Before the Committee on Aeronautical and Sciences, United States Senate." Borman presented a blunt and concise summary of the findings of the Review Board to the Senate Committee.

196

FINDING:

A. The command module contained many types and classes of combustible material in areas contiguous to possible ignition sources.

B. The test was conducted with a 16.7 pounds per square inch absolute, 100 percent oxygen atmosphere.

DETERMINATION:

The test conditions were extremely hazardous.

RECOMMENDATION:

The amount and location of combustible materials in the command module be severely restricted and controlled.

FINDING:

A. The rapid spread of fire caused an increase in pressure and temperature which resulted in rupture of the command module and creation of a toxic atmosphere. Death of the crew was from asphyxia due to inhalation of toxic gasses due to fire. A contributory cause of death was thermal burns.

B. Non-uniform distribution of carboxyhemoglobin was found by autopsy.

DETERMINATION:

Autopsy data leads to the medical opinion that unconsciousness occurred rapidly and that death followed soon thereafter.

FINDING:

Due to internal pressure, the command module inner hatch could not be opened prior to rupture of the command module.

DETERMINATION:

The crew was never capable of effecting emergency egress because of the pressurization before rupture and their loss of consciousness soon after rupture.

RECOMMENDATION:

The time required for egress of the crew be reduced and the operations necessary for egress be simplified.

FINDING:

An examination of operating practices showed the following examples of problem areas:

A. The number of open items at the time of shipment of the command module 012 was not known. There were 113 significant engineering orders not accomplished at the time command module 012 was delivered to NASA, 623 engineering orders were released subsequent to delivery of these, 22 were recent releases which were not recorded in configuration records at the time of the accident.

B. Established requirements were not followed with regard to the pre-test constraints list. The list was not completed and signed by designated contractor and NASA personnel prior to the test, even though oral agreement to proceed was reached.

C. Formulation of and changes to pre-launch test requirements for the Apollo spacecraft program were unresponsive to changing conditions.

D. Non-certified equipment items were installed in the command module at time of test.

E. Discrepancies existed between NAA and NASA MSC specifications regarding inclusion and positioning of flammable materials.

F. The test specification was released August 1966 and was not updated to include accumulated changes from release date to date of the test.

DETERMINATION:

Problems of program management and relationships between centers and with the contractors have led in some cases to insufficient response to changing program requirements.

RECOMMENDATION:

Every effort must be made to insure the maximum clarification and understanding of the responsibilities of all the organizations involved, the objective being a fully coordinated and efficient program.

That pretty much said it all. There was plenty of blame for everyone.

It was made very clear by NASA's Dr. George Mueller in answer to a question posed by a member of the Senate Space Committee that the prime responsibility for all aspects of the Apollo program was NASA's. Period.

North American Aviation's President Lee Atwood said it differently. Each of us in management associated with the Apollo program received a directive from Mr. Atwood stating that North American Aviation would accept any and all blame for the Apollo One accident. We were not to argue about any segment of responsibility for the tragedy. NASA was our customer. It was a logical move from the management standpoint, since our company had eyes on other sizable contracts with NASA on the horizon, such as a space shuttle, for example. We would accept the blame by directive from our company president.

An interesting move was made by North American within a few months following the fire on Pad 34. Each and every member of our Cape management team at my level and above was gone – fired, transferred, or invited to quit. The general manager of our Apollo operations was transferred; the managers of quality control, technicians, instrumentation, ground support equipment, project test engineering and Apollo test operations were replaced. As the Navy says, "clean sweep down fore and aft."

I took a leave of absence for a year to do some lecturing, then took early retirement from the company. For me it was a sad ending to the memorable years I spent with North American as a test pilot and as Apollo test manager in a remarkable program, which subsequently put our Americans on the moon, with my friend and squadronmate Neil Armstrong leading the way.

XII

TAILHOOK

I have been a proud member of the Tailhook Association for many years, have participated in the Association's activities, contributed articles to their fine quarterly magazine, entitled *The Hook,* and treasured my relationship with the Association and its 15,000 members. The widely publicized events which occurred in the "gauntlet" of the 1991 Tailhook symposium represent a travesty of justice.

For several years we have read about, heard about, and thought about the sexual harassment allegations associated with the Tailhook Association annual symposium of 1991, held at the Las Vegas Hilton. I have attended the symposium a number of times, as recently as 1994. I attended the panel sessions, visited the parties and yes, stood with the guys in the so-called gauntlet hallway on the third floor of the Hilton. Let me offer a different perspective from what has been published and broadcast over the past couple of years. I know what happened at the infamous '91 symposium. I was there.

First of all, sexual harassment of women there or anywhere else is unacceptable. When a woman says, "No," anytime – at a party, in a bedroom, on a street corner – she means NO and that is that. Fortunately, a vast majority of men realize and respect this. A few do not.

The Tailhook symposium is unlike any other meeting of military officers in the world. In order to be a regular member of the Association, one must have landed on Navy aircraft carriers. The Tailhookers, men and women, are a proud group of aviators and rightly so. Flying off and onto aircraft carriers in any weather, day or night, in defense of our country is a notable accomplishment. The Tailhook symposium provides an opportunity for the younger male and female carrier pilots and aircrew members to rub shoulders with the Admirals who buy the airplanes and give the orders. It also provides opportunities for them to express ideas and suggestions about their flying machines. The Admirals listen. The notorious symposium of 1991 was attended by the Secretary of the Navy, the Chief of Naval Operations and all the fleet commanders, along with many veterans of Desert Storm. It was a time for learning, sharing, and celebrating.

It should be made clear that the much maligned Tailhook Association which hosted the symposium had nothing at all to do with any of the sexual harassment events so well-publicized in the media. The Inspector General's report confirms this. The symposium was over, the panel sessions ended, the banquet completed. The third floor, west wing of the Hilton consists of rooms and suites open to all and consigned to a myriad of organizations and individuals. The Tailhook Association was not involved in the assignment of rooms, nor the guests entertained, nor anything else which occurred there. In fact, it seemed to me that half of Las Vegas was there at the 1990 and 1991 gatherings. Everyone in town knows it is a party night and they attend for various reasons.

As I stood in the gauntlet after the symposium had ended, I learned the young man next to me had never flown an airplane in his entire life. He was a croupier at a local casino. He introduced me to his friends – all young men from Las Vegas who had never seen an aircraft carrier. Everyone wore civilian clothing. No one wore a name tag.

In 1990, a Navy plane from Jacksonville transported me and about seventy other pilots and aircrew to Las Vegas. All were dressed in Navy whites. Approximately twenty-five per cent of the group were women. I spoke with one female lieutenant who had 300 carrier landings in jets. She was bright, personable, accomplished, and professional. On the entire trip I did not speak with a male Navy pilot who didn't have the utmost respect and admiration for his female counterparts. Some of the pilots had female bombardier/navigators riding beside them flying jets off carriers in the dark of night. How could you not admire and respect these women. Everyone does.

And everyone was aware of the party atmosphere at the Hilton following the symposium. In 1990 and 1991, the female officers wore their uniforms to the many parties on the third floor. They partied primarily in the patios adjoining the hospitality suites and had a blast. The so-called gauntlet, manned by Navy pilots and many others, was also the party ground for the ladies of Las Vegas who chose to attend. They were there for the "fun and games." They knew. They laughed. They giggled. They had the kind of fun they came for and nobody got hurt. Everyone knew.

In 1991, something different happened. Several female Naval officers decided to take on the guys – and they did. They appeared in civilian clothing, led by a female Navy Lieutenant who was neither a member of the Tailhook Association nor registered at the symposium. When the fun and games of the gauntlet began and these women said, "Stop!" it, by God, should have stopped immediately. When they said, "No!" to the touching and groping, it should have stopped immediately, but apparently it did not. And so the drunken aviators, drunken croupiers, drunken service station attendants – busy playing games and having fun with the ladies of the night who wanted to be there – found themselves trying to play games with women who should not have been there.

The outcome was extraordinarily regrettable. The female officers should not have been harassed. The Tailhook Association's exceptional reputation was severely tarnished. The Secretary of the Navy resigned. Several Admirals were forced to retire and others were reassigned to lesser tasks. Some pilots faced discipline charges and the 99.99 percent of the male officers (active and retired) who had nothing at all to do with the event will continue to suffer its consequences. How about the croupiers? And the service station attendants? On a satirical note, several ladies from Las Vegas reported they had been harassed more than once during a period of several days. One wonders why they kept coming back. With all the damage initiated by a few female Naval officers at the Tailhook symposium one pondered what Navy they were in.

The whistle blower in this so-called bacchanal was a Navy female helicopter pilot named Paula Coughlin, Lieutenant, United States Navy. Lieutenant Coughlin, neither a member of the Tailhook Association nor registered for the symposium, said she wandered innocently onto the third floor of the Las Vegas Hilton – the party hall – the gauntlet – and could not believe how she was treated. She was dressed in civilian clothes as were the many other ladies from Las Vegas who were there for financial gain.

Coughlin said she had never heard of the gauntlet, although this was the second Tailhook symposium she had attended at the Hilton. In both events, she was apparently an active and willing participant in the many party activities adjacent to the third floor, west wing hallway. She had her legs shaved in one suite occupied by a Navy squadron advertising free leg shaves – not once, but reportedly twice.

The bottom line, as it were, was that many of the women who walked the gauntlet on party night at the Hilton were the local ladies of the night plying their ageless trade. Everyone knew it. It happened every year, all year, not just at the Tailhook convention but also at every convention convened in Las Vegas. Whatever Coughlin's motives were, she walked off with a five million dollar settlement from the Hilton.

Paula Coughlin, with five million dollars in the bank, resigned from the U.S. Navy. She could now buy her own helicopter, maybe even her own Navy.

The post-Tailhook inquisition went on full blast for almost two years. The Navy's investigation of the matter did not find sufficient wrongdoing nor did it incriminate enough officers to satisfy the political vultures who flew close overhead. The fact that the Secretary of the Navy resigned, a number of Admirals were forced to retire, many Naval officers were suspect and would be subject to court martials was not enough.

Symbolic of the Tailhook witch hunt was the case of Commander Robert Stumpf. An eighteen-year veteran in one of the military's most dangerous and demanding professions, Stumpf was commander of the Blue Angels, the Navy's elite flight demonstration team. An F-18 pilot and Gulf War hero who had been awarded the Distinguished Flying Cross for his heroism in Desert Storm, he came to Tailhook to be honored for commanding the best fleet F-18 squadron in the Navy. But in the aftermath of the convention, he found himself removed from his Blue Angel assignment without a single charge being filed against him. His crime was to have been in a private room (NOT on the third floor of the Hilton) having cocktails with some fellow pilots thought to have been involved in the gauntlet mess.

After many months, Stumpf was rightly returned to his command. Did this hero deserve the treatment he received? Absolutely not. Thanks, Paula.

One of the principle topics of discussion at the symposium was whether women pilots should be permitted to fly in combat. Like many male aviators, I feel strongly that women should not fly in combat if there is a

chance they might be shot down and captured. It has nothing to d
whether they are capable of flying combat missions. You're damn rigl
are. They can do the job just as well as their male counterparts. Bu
would they be subjected to if they were captured and housed in some
like the Hanoi Hilton for five years or so? Just ask former Senato1
Denton, Senator John McCain, Admiral Jim Stockdale, or Colonel John
among those who spent more than five years imprisoned during th(
nam War. They were only beaten, had arms and legs broken, teeth kn
out. What would have been done to a woman prisoner in those circumst:
How many times a day can a woman be raped before she dies – or v
she were dead?

Lieutenant Coughlin was a strong advocate of women being al
to fly in combat and was heard arguing her position vehemently the I
evening before the wrong stuff hit the fan the next night. She was quo
the *Los Angeles Times*: "I look at many of these guys – who still don't g
and I think to myself, 'It WAS their Navy. It's soon going to be my genera
Navy.'"

If Paula was trying to make her point Saturday night, she did.
Coughlin is not in the Navy now and will not have the opportunity
shot down, and captured.

The price for Tailhook has been appalling for everyone – the
the military in general, Admirals, civil servants, Naval aviators, an
Tailhook Association itself in spite of its being held blameless for the ‹
day night events. I attended the 1993 symposium in San Diego, the firs
vened since the 1991 debacle. At the symposium were three Congress
Medal of Honor winners, several retired Admirals who led our Naval f
to victory in the Pacific during World War II, and a heroic Navy Ca
who had his right arm shot off in aerial combat over Vietnam yet m:
back flying with his left arm. He is now affectionately known as "Ca
Hook".

Also among those in attendance was one of the Navy's top c
pilots who had made more that 350 carrier landing in daylight and
ness. She was then a Lieutenant Commander now a Commander, U
States Navy.

The Tailhook Association will survive. Membership dropped
about 15,000 to 13,500 as an aftermath of Tailhook '91, but the numbe:

climbing again, and corporate members are quietly rejoining for a good reason. The membership is comprised of the elite military pilots of the world, those men and women who fly off and onto aircraft carriers, and those corporations that build their flying machines.

Good-bye, Paula Coughlin. We shall not miss you in Naval aviation.

XIII

MARILYNN

She was the most beautiful girl/woman I ever saw – ever. She was delicate; she had the elegance of a movie queen; she was gentle. Her femininity was pure grace; her presence enchanted a room when she entered; and for reasons I never quite understood, she loved me.

Marilynn and I were engaged just prior to my entering the Naval Aviation Cadet program, and she was the light at the end of the flight training tunnel, which shone on the Navy Wings of Gold and two golden wedding bands. We were married in 1945, and during our twenty-one years together, she gave me four wonderful children – three great boys and a beautiful little girl who is almost a mirror image of her mom.

During our first three years of marriage, Ensign John Moore, Navy pilot, was stationed at seven different bases and we lived in fourteen different apartments. We had been married a year before we bought a car – a 1937 Ford with a zillion miles on it – all we could afford on my $275 a month paycheck, which included flight pay for flying F6F Hellcats.

We bought the car from a Marine at NAS Vero Beach, Florida, and Marilynn noticed that none of the gauges on the dashboard worked – zero fuel indicated, zero oil pressure, zero generator charge – and she was curious about it.

"How do you know these things work?" she asked.

"Because," I replied, "the guy said everything worked and if you can't trust a Marine, who can you trust?"

"Right," she said gently with a warm smile, hiding some doubt about the whole deal.

The next day, we packed the car and headed south to our new station, NAS Key West, for night fighters. About thirty miles into the venture, the Ford ground to a halt at the side of the road. The engine had frozen. No oil pressure. Marilynn never said a word – no "I told you so," no "dumb ass," no "blockhead." I wondered why she didn't just get out and take a bus back to St. Louis. What a lady she was!

My mother came to visit us at Key West where we had rented a one room efficiency apartment. No place for Mother to sleep except in our double bed, with us, where she slept in the middle, "in order to be close to both of you," she said. Marilynn and I shared the opposite edges of the bed. Marilynn never complained. After a week of this Mom-imposed celibacy, we put her on a bus headed northward then hurried home to make love.

Over the years, Marilynn was a loving wife and mother. She took in stride my flying off aircraft carriers day and night, getting shot at, getting burned to a crisp, being a test pilot – always supportive, always caring, always there.

When I was Manager of Apollo Test Operations at the Kennedy Space Center, living in Cocoa Beach, Florida, we took time away from the world to spend a week's vacation in the Florida Keys with our four children, aged eight to eighteen years. A 1966 memorable trip in so many ways – sun, water, fishing, swimming pool, lobster, and then the trip home.

We were fifteen miles from Cocoa Beach in our station wagon, towing our sixteen-foot boat, two of us in the front seat, two in the middle, and Marilynn and eight year old Larry in the back seat (no seat belts there). Suddenly, there was a terrific impact from behind us. I glanced quickly into the rear view mirror to see a green sedan smashing into the rear end of our station wagon. The boat was already gone. We had been struck from the rear by a drunken driver doing eighty miles an hour, causing our car to careen into a wild skid sideways across the highway into on-coming traffic. There was a second extraordinary impact as an on-coming vehicle struck the right rear of the station wagon.

The next I heard was Larry screaming from outside the car, "Mommy! Mommy! Mommy!" I looked into the back of the car and saw the side window ripped out and Marilynn and Larry gone. I raced around to the right side of the car and found this lovely woman who never hurt anyone, lying on the road, her throat slit by window glass, and her beautiful, big, gentle heart rapidly pumping all the blood out of her body in foot-high gushes. I took her in my arms and held her helplessly as the last of her blood was pumped onto the highway and she died in my arms as our four children stood by sobbing.

There was an extraordinary finality to this tragic moment as an ambulance crew took Marilynn gently from my arms and put her in a body bag and zipped it closed...

It was not supposed to end this way. I was the one who would die first, testing airplanes or getting shot up in combat. No harm would ever come to one so gentle, so loving, so very beautiful, as was she.

We, the five of us, chose these words to mark her resting place under a majestic oak tree, there to look over her, always.

Marilynn Moore

1923 - 1966

So Very Beautiful

EPILOGUE

Marilynn's tragic death was devastating. Our heartache and pain were not unique but certainly well understood by those in our world who have lost loved ones as suddenly and as dramatically as we had lost this beautiful woman. They say that "life goes on," and it does, but not easily.

The children, ages eighteen, fifteen, thirteen and eight, were very close to their grandmother, Marilynn's mother, who was kind enough to move down and into our home from Jacksonville to provide some stability in the family. At this time, I was working six and seven days a week at the Cape preparing for the first manned launch of an Apollo Spacecraft, Apollo One. Without "Gram" I don't know how we would have made it through those very difficult times.

It was only five months after we lost Marilynn that our nation lost three men admired, three idols, three more loved ones in the Apollo One Command Module fire on Pad 34. I watched helplessly from the control room. Often I have reflected on the realization that the pain and heartache felt from the tragic losses over those five months were far more acute than the physical pain I remembered from having been badly burned and blown off the flight deck and into the sea during the Korean War.

As told earlier (Chapter Eleven) I was relieved of my "command" shortly after the Pad 34 tragedy and my company's plan was that I be transferred to Palmdale, California, to support the flight test planning effort related to the B-70 bomber, which was soon to be born from North American Aviation's womb. Considering the upheaval in my personal life I could not condone such a major move with its potential trauma to my family, and I consequently declined NAA's gracious offer to move us from our Cocoa Beach home to California.

I instead took a leave of absence from NAA, which was then transitioning into North American Rockwell (subsequently Rockwell International). In this period, I lectured at universities and conventions nationwide on space related subjects, enjoying the hospitality of such fine institutions as Dartmouth, UCLA, Auburn, Georgia Tech, and University of Missouri among others. But then travel was not helpful to my family life, and so I subsequently terminated my lecturing career and at the same time retired from Rockwell.

Some years after Marilynn's death, I met and married a lovely young woman named Joan Wright, from San Diego. She was seventeen years my junior but fit into my family like a glove. In this time period my oldest son Randy was with the 101st Airborne unit headed for Vietnam. Son David was a paratrooper with an Army Med evac unit and had made five parachute jumps more than I had ever made (my total: none). Beautiful daughter Anne was attending the University of South Florida in Tampa, and the youngest of the gang, Larry, then age twelve, was crashing the pubic barrier like Chuck Yeager did Mach I.

Shortly after Joan and I married, we set up and owned a small business manufacturing, of all things, waterbeds: The Florida Waterbed Corporation. We designed them, we made them, we sold them nationwide. A lot of folks laughed at us and our venture, but in the ten years that we owned the small company we grossed more than seven million dollars. That will put your kids through college, buy a new car, and allow us older guys to bust our asses on the slopes of Aspen, Colorado.

In the evolution of becoming a small businessman, however, I became disenchanted with the encumbrances of city government, which spent a lot of energy telling me what I could not do and very little telling me what I could do or helping me in my enterprise. So I decided to do something about it.

In 1975, I ran for and was elected Mayor of the city of Cocoa Beach, a lovely small beach-side community of about 12,000 permanent residents, a number which swelled to 20,000 when the condo owners came home to escape the northern winter weather. I learned a lot of things rather quickly about mayorhood:

1.   Not everybody likes what you are trying to do.

2.   You only hear from the people with the gripes.

3.   You cut a lot of ribbons.

4.   You may be the glorious leader, but you only have one vote on the commission (we had five commissioners).

5.   A few very vocal citizens can generate a lot of influence on city government, good and bad.

6.   The Mayor needs to be able to turn off his telephone at bedtime. I had been mayor for almost a week when some guy called in the middle of the night complaining bitterly about dogs barking on the beach and insisting that I do something about it immediately. I got dressed and went down to the beach and could not hear a single doggie yelp. The next day I had a switch put on my phone and for the next three years got no calls after bedtime. Some months after the dog barking call, I learned that the caller had been my great friend Admiral Bob Baldwin who was calling from California!

After three years in office, I concluded that I was destined for bigger things and set my sights on becoming El Presidente of the U.S. of A, via our House of Representatives, then the Senate, and then by acclamation, the White House.

I abdicated the Mayor's office after one glorious term to begin my quest for the holiest grail in our country, by way of our House of Representatives. I did truly run a remarkable campaign and was rewarded by coming in second in my race for the House. Unfortunately, it was a two man race. My getting 49.5% of the votes was laudable, but not quite good enough. So much for my political aspirations. It was our country's loss, Joan kept telling me.

Today I fly just enough to be dangerous. My friend Palmer Bannerot of Valencia, Pennsylvania, has a late model Cessna 310 that he lets me fly from the right seat, except that while I am flying he never lets loose of the wheel on his side. Makes it hard to turn.

My college mate and life-long friend, Morris Sievert, who lives in La Jolla with his lovely wife La Wanda (I was at their wedding fifty three years ago), and I get together several times a year on fishing ventures. We try to spend several weeks each summer fishing in Islamorada in the Florida Keys with the Ginestras from Ft. Lauderdale, the Bannerots from Pennsylvania, and the Hoffmanns from Chicago. We also spend a week each summer fishing from a houseboat on Lake Powell with a group we call the Senile Six. Not everyone is senile, only three of us.

Joan and I slowly grew apart and were divorced several years ago. She is now an executive with a large company in San Diego and we remain good friends. Son Randy, now 47, is a highly decorated Vietnam veteran who returned from the war, put himself through college, put himself through law school at the University of Florida (with honors), and is now the Chief Trial Lawyer in the felony division of our Public Defender's office. Randy has a seven-year-old daughter, Laura, who is a charmer.

Son David, 45, is an administrator in the Law Enforcement system in Gainesville, Florida, and lives with his delightful wife Dot, a nurse, and two gorgeous daughters, each of whom marches to a 3.95 scholastic average in high school.

My daughter Anne, in her early forties, is completely beautiful, looks just like her mom. She is an assistant Manager of a Post Office Branch in Tampa and is the love of my life.

Son Larry, now 38, is a nationally acclaimed designer/illustrator who has had contracts with Disney, Sea World, and a number of national business chains such as Publix Markets and the Olive Branch restaurant. He is married to Nancy, a Vice President of Nations Bank. They all graduated from college, with or without my help. Good genes; Thank you, Marilynn, for all you provided.

Finally, if you have made it this far as a reader of *The Wrong Stuff* I want to thank you for your perseverance, for letting me share some of my personal life with you, and for being indulgent with my sentiments about my family. I promise not to write any more books or crash any more airplanes.

John Moore